Swell

Swell

A Girl's Guide to the Good Life

Cynthia Rowley & Ilene Rosenzweig

WARNER BOOKS

A Time Warner Company

Copyright © 1999 by Cynthia Rowley and Ilene Rosenzweig

All rights reserved.

Warner Books, Inc., 1271 Avenue of the Americas, New York, NY 10020

Visit our Web site at www.warnerbooks.com

Ⓦ A Time Warner Company

Printed in the United States of America

First Printing: October 1999

10 9 8 7 6 5

Library of Congress Cataloging-in-Publication Data

Rowley, Cynthia. Swell : a girl's guide to the good life / Cynthia Rowley and Ilene Rosenzweig.

p. cm.

ISBN 0-446-52456-5

1. Women—United States —Life skills guides. 2. Teenage girls—United States—Life skills guides.

3. Women—Psychology. 4. Success.   I. Rosenzweig, Ilene. II.Title.

HQ1221.R747 1999   99-24242

646.7'0082—dc21   CIP

We'd like to thank all the people who helped squeeze out this book. Rick Marin, a swell writer and special pallie who read and offered suggestions from the proposal to the finish line, and who contributed a ton to the voice of this book. Debra Rosenzweig, who helped heaps with the final draft. Bill Keenan, a swell daddy and muse. Our patient editor, Caryn Karmatz Rudy. Binky—The Agent—Urban. And all the friends, family, and swell heroes who make cameos in these pages. Any resemblance in this book to *Swell* characters, living or dead, is purely intentional.

What's Inside

What a Life, What a Word!

Welcome to our little book about livin' big—

Swell is a style compass for the girl on the go. It's a guide to navigating the world with a little swagger and a lot of grace. Because making things look easy isn't as easy as it looks—a girl's gotta know a trick or two. Like how to "duke" a maître d' to get a good table, throw an emergency dinner party, con the shy guy into taking your number. All that stuff no one ever taught you—but you wish they had—unless your mom went to charm school in Vegas.

The swell girl doesn't have to have tons of time on her hands or dough in her purse to be a big tipper, a big romantic, throw big parties—even for two—or to think about the big picture and what she'll wear to the premiere. A swell is a bonne vivante, but not a snob. She's witty, wily, and plenty smooth. She's the original 21st Century Fox.

Swell is the place where spirit and style meet. We wanted to write about joie de vivre—only less French. So we went with the all-American translation—*Swell!*—and mixed in a few tales of our own with examples from the lives of our swell heroes Audrey Hepburn, Frank Sinatra, Lucille Ball, James Bond—anyone with a lotta largesse, plenty of polish, and an appetite for adventure, screwball or suave.

The nine chapters in this book swing from high to low. From truffles to deviled eggs. From Dean Martin's hangover cure to the fine art of squeezing your entire life into a four-inch purse to foolproof techniques for climbing into a cab in a pencil skirt without flashing panty. Our idea of polite society isn't where to put the soup spoons. It's more about gallantry and chivalry, and raiding from the other side all those magnanimous traits of manhood that make old black-and-white movies so sexy. Why can't a girl be the sport who shows up with flowers on a first date? Not that she's afraid to show her feminine side and write love letters while wearing her maribou slippers. The swell samples the best from all worlds. Old, young. Boy, girl. Fancy, trashy. Her own modern idea of cool is big enough to include even "uncool" fun: family vacations, a "welcome home" message scrawled in chalk on the sidewalk , or reading a book called "A girl's guide to the good life."

Now let's get this party started!

7

Swell

1 Break Some Eggs
Enter the imperfect hostess

There's a reason they call it throwing a party. Things break, you gotta be ready for a few curve balls: caterers who don't show up; unexpected guests who do. And the best bashes have your own special spin. We're not talking about spinning sugar into Eiffel Tower pralines either. Who's got that kind of time?

The parties that really take off are often the ones that come together at the last minute. That's when the best ideas happen—in a flash of inspiration, a burst of spontaneous combustion. Maybe it's a picnic in your apartment. Christmas lights in July. Burnt roast? Skip from salad to three dessert courses. If it "just isn't done," do it anyway. People get caught up in some idea of how things are supposed to be. Forget that. Not enough soup spoons? Let 'em slurp. A party is like theater: intimate, live, anything can happen. That's the thrill of it. The key is to keep the show going at all costs, to see disasters as challenges to your improvisational skills, and gaffes as memorable moments. Besides, what if everything goes right? Your problem will be even worse—a perfect party that swings about as hard as a charity luncheon. Perfection is overrated.

Enter the Imperfect Hostess. She celebrates quirks, takes risks, courts mayhem, and what she lacks in resources and time, she makes up for with ingenuity, her speed-dial, and the Pretty Good Housekeeping Seal of Approval.

Cupcakes on Your Wedding Day

Cynthia: *I had the Who all settled, now I had to figure out the Where. We couldn't just have it in some boring hotel where they'd probably already churned out twelve weddings that day. We wanted to find a place that was us. Adventure Playland? The Empire State Building! (If only Aunt Agnes didn't have a fear of heights.) A bowling alley? (Bad lighting.) I just wanted to marry the guy—and for our friends to have a good time. Then I thought, City Hall!*

Now that might seem kinda conventional, but we customized it. I convinced the mayor's office to let us hang a Cynthia and Bill 4Ever banner from the second floor windows, and Bill's Uncle Jean played the Wedding March on his accordion. Then we took a Checker cab with a Just Married sign out to an airstrip in Brooklyn at Floyd Bennett Field, where Bill's dad used to chopper out on his special cop missions. A forty-thousand-square-foot hangar that hadn't been used since the forties was about as far from a wedding hall as you could get. There were some problems, like no electricity, no plumbing, pigeons in the rafters. But how often do you get to use a DC3 as a centerpiece?

It was a bit rough, but we dressed it up. We handed out boarding cards with seating assignments to the arriving guests. There were no fancy floral arrangements, just tons of sunflowers— they reminded us of Italy, where Bill proposed—in metal garden buckets from the flea market, arranged down the center of a mile-long table covered with a bolt of white cotton fabric. (I hate splitting people up into tables; this was more like one big happy family.) I wrote love poems in Magic Marker down the middle. Each personal touch made it feel more romantic. Even the cake. Have you ever heard that if you sleep with a piece of wedding cake under your pillow, you'll dream of the one you'll marry? Well, neither had I. But when we did, we wanted all our guests to have their own cake, so we stacked the dessert table with a couple hundred cupcakes, each topped with a bride and groom. As for the bouquet, I don't even like carrying a handbag, so I wasn't too eager to be lugging around a bunch of lilies all day and night. I got out of it by putting a small spray in a lipstick tote. Much more important to have my hands free at all times—to give my honey a squeeze.

MAKE BIG PARTIES SMALL . . .

Whether it's a wedding for two hundred or a dinner for two, keep it personal. Mix the traditional with the unconventional, the formal with the informal, the caviar with the deviled eggs. Follow your own tastes even if they don't seem to go together. The modern affair is a freestyle event, and one where you remember more than just whether you had the chicken or the fish.

Jumping New Year's

Ilene: It was New Year's Eve minus twelve hours. No party. I called Cynthia: "Where's the action?" "No action," she said. Nothing like the pressure of a big night to suck the party spirit right out of you. Dressing up, getting stuck in traffic at Times Square, eating a pricey prix-fixe dinner. Who needs it? Not to mention I didn't have a date. Things were looking bleak. And it wasn't getting any earlier.

Time for emergency measures. With no plan A we skipped to plan B. Evacuate the city, head for the hills. Up the river to Cynthia's house. "I've got the grapes, you bring the fish," said Cynthia, "for good luck. And don't forget to wear yellow underwear." It's good luck, too. I hit the specialty shop running: caviar, crème fraîche, smoked trout and salmon, beet salad, cucumber slaw. Who knew fish could eat such a big hole in your pocket? I'll pay the bills next year! By the time I arrived, with a few friends in tow, it was dark and snowing. No going home that night, "but plenty of good sledding down the driveway," said Cynthia. There being no sled, the pan of Bill's wheelbarrow had to serve as luge. Once inside, our skin on fire with defrost, we broke out the noisemakers, put the champagne on ice in a top hat, and got cozy with a hot fire and the cold supper. For good luck, we each ate twelve grapes and someone threw a bucket of cold water out the window. By 11:00, suitably tipsy, we went around the room and tried to remember the year's brightest moments and darkest hours. At 11:45 all was well when someone yelled: "I want to be in midair at the stroke of midnight." It came from Cynthia, already a blur, hurling parkas and mittens out of the closet. The big hand but an inch from 12:00, we were bundled up again, jogging through the snow, champagne spilling out of the go-cups. But by midnight we made it to the trampoline! Jumping up at the stars. That's what I call living the high life.

Not everything has to be a production planned weeks in advance. "In and out, nobody gets hurt." The last-minute blast is a matter of knowing which corners to cut, how to make do with what you've got. It's all in the packaging.

SHORT-ORDER COOKING

Take-Out Surprise

The surprise is...they don't know it's take-out.

Who says having a dinner party means you do all the cooking? Veteran take-out artists know there's no shame in self-catering. Call 1-800-Hot-Hams and have them overnight you a honey-glazed beauty straight from a Virginia smokehouse. Or, decant a few Family Packs of KFC. In the bucket it looks like fast food. But put it in a basket lined with a red-checked cloth and some sprigs of thyme, and your finger-lickin' guests will swear you've been sweating over a fryer since sunup. Let'em. So long as it looks good and goes down easy. Remember this homey trinity: Keep the lighting low. Garnish. Get rid of the evidence!

The Quick-and-Dirty Dinner Party

Dinner at eight for six, and you're leaving the office at five. Gotta think fast. Speeding home in a manic panic, menus flash through your mind's eye. But there's no time to cook, barely time to shop.

Whip through the grocery like a supermarket sweepstakes contestant: two chickens (nothing's simpler than roast chicken, especially if someone else already did the roasting), a quick stop at the cheese counter for a couple of goat logs, a Sara Lee cheesecake (you'll see), baby carrots and newborn spuds (everything little cooks faster and looks cuter). Pillage the produce section not just for salad but anything pretty that could pass for a garnish. Parsley, mint, rosemary, grapes, berries, pomegranates, baby apples. Overbuy. Don't worry, you're gonna need it.

You're home. The clock is ticking, you've got fifty-nine minutes to make it look like you've been toiling all day. Oven on: 350. Hurl potatoes and carrots into a roasting pan, drizzle with olive oil and plenty of salt and pepper. Go to the goat cheese. Treat like Play-Doh. Flatten two logs, then cut into the shape of a heart and transplant to a plate. If it breaks, don't cry, mush cracks together. Chop cherry tomatoes—or sundried tomatoes if you've got 'em—or anything red, and spread over the top. Get it out to the coffee table pronto.

Oops. Forgot the bread. Search for crackers. Fail to find. Resort to stale loaf of white bread. Cut into triangles. The oven's already on; throw 'em on a cookie sheet for five minutes and voilà! Wonder Melba Points. Now lose those chicken bags and the Sara Lee box. Uh-oh. Birds look like they died of boredom. Bring back to life with a fistful of rosemary before letting 'em roost with the potatoes and carrots. Just long enough for some herbal aromatherapy. Salad: Waldorf it by chopping walnuts and baby apples (leave one whole on the side of each salad plate). Doorbell rings. Hey! It's only ten to eight. So much for showering and changing. No option but to pretty up with a clean apron, lipstick—and pearls? Kiss kiss, clink clink. Just when you're starting to get happy, the guests are clamoring for dessert.

Alrighty then. Back to the trenches. You've got one more round of ammo. Sit the Sara Lee on a plate. Rinse a pint of blueberries, empty into a pan. Sprinkle with a teaspoon of sugar. Melt over low flame. Then pour over the cake, letting the blue goo drip down the sides. (Messy looks homemade.) For extra credit: Split the cheesecake horizontally by pulling a piece of dental floss through. Remove the top layer, pour the blue goo on the bottom layer. Replace top layer and cover with another box of berries, uncooked.

When the jaw-dropped guests shout, "You made this?" smile back and remind yourself, "Yeah. I made it *good*."

Other Fast Fixes

Don't have enough (or any) serving platters . . .

With minor cosmetic surgery and well-placed shrubbery, the chipped plate or beat-up cutting board will pinch hit for Wedgwood. A little green goes a long way: line any potential serving tray with overlapping fans of lettuce leaves, a carpet of dill, or a wreath of basil spilling over the edges. Not too neat, or people will be expecting rose-cut tomatoes and origami radishes. Food, like a face, can be scary if it looks too "done."

The frittata broke in half . . .

Trim the edges, and present it in two pieces on a bed of parsley with a few daisies planted down the divide.

The chocolate layer cake comes out like the Tower of Pisa . . .

Stick a half-moon of sparklers in the sloping side, and—ba-da-bing—a cake they can't refuse.

There's a paw print in the pie . . .

Slice the untrampled remainder into eight neat wedges, arrange in a circle, then plop a box of cherries into the middle and let them fill up the gaps.

365 Excuses for a Party

Birthdays, Fourth of July, and things that happen in December aren't the only time for champagne and fireworks. What are you waiting for? Every day's a holiday—for someone, somewhere. Adopt one! There's always a reason to have a party tomorrow.

12 Steps to Getting in Touch with Your Inner Holidays

January 3: The planet Mercury is visible. Roof party! Rent a telescope and an astrologer, serve Tang.

February 2: Groundhog Day. Have a dinner party; after dessert serve appetizers all over again.

March 14: Anniversary of Canada's constitution. Fry up the bacon, put the Molson on ice, all sentences must be finished with "eh?" Bonus quiz question: Name the capital of Canada. Answer: "Ottawa, eh?"

April 28: Arbor Day. (Lead your party on a hike; fill canteens with "sap"—a wicked potion of your creation that only a sap would drink.)

May 6: Anniversary of the purchase of Manhattan by Peter Minuit. Serve Manhattans, clam chowder, and top your CD playlist with "New York, New York" by Frank.

June 8: Birthday of Cole Porter. Bring your p.j.'s. Time for a night and day party.

June 21: First day of summer. Indoor beach party—blankets on the floor, beach balls, umbrellas, drinks in coolers, and lots of self-tanner.

August 16: Day Elvis died. Hand out fake sideburns, play "Blue Suede Shoes." Serve fried peanut butter-and-banana sandwiches—everything gets fried, including the guests.

September 1: Oyster season begins. Wear pearls, down oyster shooters, have everyone bring their favorite aphrodisiac.

October 10: Alaska Day. Turn the heat off, use earmuffs as napkin rings; make baked Alaska, rub noses.

November 4: The Facts of Life canceled anniversary. Everybody brings fattest picture of themselves from adolescence; serve binge food, like Snow Balls, Doritos, cheese fries; encourage group rap sessions.

December 17: Anniversary of the Wright brothers' first takeoff. Serve in-flight peanut packages and mile-high club sandwiches; play musical chairs between first-class and coach seating at the dinner table.

JUNK MAIL AND OTHER INVITATIONS

Crane's stationery is really nice, but invitations don't all have to be that stiff. As long as it's got the where and when, who cares how heavy the paper stock is?

Other Ways to Put Your Own Stamp on an Invitation

For a drinks party, a cocktail napkin—with lipstick on it.

It's a s'prise: A mock ransom note: "We have [your friend's name here] captive. If you want to see [your friend's name here] alive again, meet us at [where and when]. Do not attempt to contact [your friend's name here]. Or you will kill the s'prise."

A white sock: For the birthday of a friend who's famous for wearing 'em with black shoes.

A doily: For a dessert party.

For when you want new blood, a chain letter: Mail each guest three chains to send to three friends with instructions that they'll be required for admittance.

Matchbox: For a bonfire, a barbecue, or any other smokin' soirée.

THE DELINQUENT DECORATOR

How to turn your shack into a palace—at least while the tiki torches are still burning

You're lying on your back, wondering how you're gonna bring your friends over to this old dump again and not make it seem like Dullsville, USA, pop. 35. Time to think vertically. Get into your mood elevator, and take the express up to the penthouse with the sunken living room, the gleaming wet bar, and the glittering 360-degree skyline view.

Okay, so your window looks out on a brick wall. You can still get that top-floor twinkle. And you don't have to scout the flea market at dawn hunting precious bric-a-brac for your dinner table. Sleep in. With a few sleights of hand—strategic cover-ups, and a creative reinterpretation of stuff from your closet—your place will feel brand-new.

Kill the Overheads

You can't have drama, romance, and mystery in a place that's brighter than a hospital waiting room. Replace the big bulb with lots of little ones. Make the hallway a runway with luminary bags guiding guests to your door. Inside, get screwy with different-colored bulbs: String white Christmas lights around the buffet table; no one likes squinting to see if that black speck on the canapé is a raisin or a fly. Candles don't have to shout ashram fest if they're treated with a twist, like a coat-hanger candelabra, or tea lights lined up on the window sills and sashes—your own faux flickering cityscape.

Staging the Scene

Think off-Broadway—way off. That makes you the director—and the production designer. You're not stuck with the everyday props in your apartment. Break down your old set and build a new one. Roll up the carpet and lay down sod if you feel so inclined. Clean off a wall and have a slide show—every guest brings one to show and tell. Whatever you don't own, and can't afford to buy, rent. Extra glassware and coat racks aren't the only things you can find in the Yellow Pages. For the same money you might blow on flower arrangements, the nearby landscaper might loan you a few topiaries for the night. But steer clear of Andrew Lloyd Weber syndrome. Hints of far-flung locations are enough: a few exotic artifacts, or evocative souvenirs. And not everything has to be so matchy. For Halloween, hang a jack-o-lantern disco ball and a velvet rope, make a VIP room out of your bedroom, and you've got Studio 54 in Hell. For a friend who's gambling on a new career, re-create the high-rolling glory days of Old Havana with rented conga drums, a slot machine, and exploding cigars. Babaloo!

Co-opting the Neighbors

Nothing puts a kabosh on a buzz faster than complaints from noisephobic neighbors. So if your jam is gonna make the neighbors deaf, alert them in advance—with an invitation stuffed under the door.

Ready, Set, Table

Lack of Irish linen is no excuse for avoiding having people for a sit-down. Why get so serious? A bare table is only half dressed, but how you cover it is up for grabs: road maps with a globe as centerpiece or just plain paper with the guests' names scrawled at their places. Napkin rings can be key chains, bowties, plastic watches. For an off-centerpiece arrange a bouquet of framed baby pictures: Each guest brings one and has to guess who's who. Or build a mountain of penny candy; lay out dice, a deck of cards, kazoos, Legos, yo-yo's, you name it.

BOOZING

The mark of a swell hostess is she knows how to have a good time at her own party—but not *too* good. She's got to stay just this side of tipsy, to keep the party in motion without getting a case of the spins. Learn your limit at other people's parties. At your own, be on your toes to lead the conga line.

Claim One of These Signature Libations as Your Own

The Hamilton (as in George Hamilton). Over ice, a shot of tequila, half a shot of rose's lime juice, and three shots cranberry juice and a lime twist. You get a tan just drinking one.

Jack and Water (as in Daniel's, Frank Sinatra's daily dose.)

Vodka Gimlet (Ilene's weakness). Two parts vodka, two parts Rose's lime juice, teaspoon of sugar and a lime twist. Straight up in a martini glass—or not at all.

Mixology 101

Ice. The bartender's best friend. Never add ice to a drink. Always pour liquor over the ice. For shaken drinks, start with pre-chilled glasses. If there isn't time or space to cool them in the fridge, fill them with ice (preferably crushed) and let them shiver while you mix the drinks in a shaker. Then dump the ice, and pour. Pour smoothly, like you mean it, finishing with a quick decisive turn of the hand. No limp wrists, no sloppy dripping. And when serving wine, never let the neck of the bottle rest on the lip of the glass.

Signature Cocktail

Cynthia: My Aunt Bonnie is famous for her three-bean salad. She makes it every time people come over, no matter what the occasion or what else she's putting out, and all the folks in Barrington always look forward to it. Everyone should have a crowd pleaser. Mine is the Mojito, the lethal Cuban cocktail: rum, sugar, crushed mint, and a splash of soda. There's nothing to it, but it knocks 'em dead, especially when you bring all the ingredients to a friend's house and mix up a batch.

Wagon Riders

Any party is bound to have some guests who've either sworn off the sauce or never got on it. That's no reason to make them feel uncomfortable. Never say, with a slurred voice, "Oh, come on, have a *real* drink." When rattling off the list of available whistle whetters, make a habit of mentioning the "dry drinks," too—tomato juice, Diet Coke, etc. A sober Sally is handy to have around as a designated driver—to make a booze run for the rest of you bums later.

Hangover Remedies

Short of abstinence and sane drinking, the best medicine for morning-after misery is preventative. For God's sake, eat something beforehand, and not just a handful of Goldfish. Before tucking in, swallow two aspirin and as much water as you can hold. Then you won't be making the fuzzy-tongue sick call to work the next morning. For a hardcore hangover, there is no cure, but there is a solution: a wondrous elixir called the Ramos Gin Fizz. Big at the Sands Hotel, back in the good days, this legendary New Orleans mix of lemon juice, egg white, powdered sugar, orange flower water, cream, and gin topped with soda was passed around on trays by the dozen to the wounded after a bender. If that don't do it, nothing will. Except maybe a malted and a steam, Dean Martin's way up off the floor.

> ### You've had a few too many if
> - The boys in blue show up at the door and you kiss them hello.
> - You remark how strange it is you'd never noticed that the skirt you're wearing has a slit in the front.
> - You hear someone else saying, "Those are my pajamas."
> - You blot your lipstick on the bathroom mirror
> - You hear yourself saying "You're my best friend." More than once.

IS EVERYBODY HAPPY?

The swell hostess aspires to make people feel at home, whether she's putting them up for the weekend, throwing a wild one, or taking her mob out to their favorite restaurant.

Working the Room

A party's like a shark. If it doesn't keep moving it dies. Circulation keeps the blood flowing, yours and your guests'. Put the bar at one end of the room and the food at the other. That'll keep 'em commuting back and forth. When the subliminal hostess orchestrates the fun, no one even notices she's doing it. To alert the guests that it's time to move into the dining room, she does not bellow "Dinner!" or frantically signal people like she's working the tarmac at O'Hare airport. Better to just flip the lights once or twice, like theater intermission. Keep an eye out for stragglers. When you spot some lonely mug taking inventory of your bookshelves, don't go over and ask "Is everything okay?" Like that's gonna help. Better to take him under your wing. Deputize him: "Sammy, do me a favor, doll. Ask that cutie if you could freshen up her drink. I've got to put out some fires in the kitchen." Or if everybody's cliqued off except the chick doing laps around the living room, give her a reason to meet people. When serving dessert, ask her to do the honors. Even the mouse in the house can handle "Did you get cake?" The best way to get the wallflowers, or anybody, talking is to make introductions that give them something to

Hitting the Spot

A swell hostess is not the type to chase after guests with ashtrays and coasters. When some nut pulls an Exxon Valdez on her new shag, she tells herself, there is no use crying over spilt Beaujolais. Try a sprinkle of salt to absorb the offending grape, then a once-over with some seltzer. Scotchgard everything. Party now, clean later. A few life-saving antidotes:

- Coffee or tea: Douse with club soda.
- Ink: Shpritz with hair spray.
- Blood spot: Mix meat tenderizer and water into a paste, let sit a half hour, then rinse.
- Spaghetti sauce: Sprinkle with baby powder to absorb grease, or clean with a squeeze of lemon.
- Bubble gum: Freeze with ice, then peel off.
- Red wine: White wine.
- Fruit stains: Boiling water.
- Red juices: Soak in milk.

work with. Don't just go "Bob, Sue; Sue, Bob," and walk away. Spread around the effusive flattery. "This is Legendary Golf Guy, Matt. He revolutionized my short game." Or, "Meet Christophe, his accent'll make your knees weak."

Bums, Slobs, and Bores

Friends date. Relatives marry. There is no accounting for the bland and unsavory characters who will be loosed upon your home once you open the door. Get ready.

Unexpected guests?

Put out more plates, get busy cooking, cut the roast into smaller portions. Your hospitality knows no bounds. If they're friends of friends, give them the benefit of the doubt. They may turn out to be future friends of yours.

A Chocolate on the Couch Pillow

Cynthia: Whenever someone's coming to stay over at my house, I try to make a little event out of it. If you're picking up your parents at the train station, put a sign on the back of the car. You want to give that four-star feeling. A guest book of dreams (and nightmares) next to the flower and pitcher of cold water on the night table, a purloined Do Not Disturb sign, and always a chocolate on the pillow—even if they're sleeping on the couch.

Handling drunks

When there's a boozy Suzy teetering dangerously on her heels, or some bombed Bob having a heated discussion with your Picasso poster, be thoughtful. Offer to freshen their drink, don't take no for an answer. Then, in the kitchen, toss the margarita and refill with a soda, sugar, and grapefruit juice, any libation of the virgin variety. For the sake of your guests and your carpet, steer them out of harm's way. Into the bedroom perhaps—for a little lie-down. You'll need a lure: "Let's have a drink in here," or "You've *got* to come inside and see my lava lamp collection."

Breakage

Guests aren't the only things that get smashed at a swell party. Expect casualties. You can't fall to pieces because your new soup tureen just did. You'll buy another one. Think of the klutzy pallie who probably feels bad enough already. If it's your grandmother's antique Rosenthal gravy boat that just capsized and you're tempted to burst into tears? That's when you need a few recovery lines in your pocket: "I've been looking for a reason to get a new one of those." Or, to vent without venom, when someone shatters one of your two brandy snifters, launch the other against the wall and say, "Now it's a matched set."

Rolling up the welcome mat

The party's over but some of your guests haven't heard the news. Time for an eviction notice, issued with finesse. Make a pot of coffee—when people smell it they get the idea. Give the Velcro guests a new destination. They'll be more likely to leave if they have somewhere to go. "Hey, kids, the air in here's getting stale. I know a dive on the corner with a great juke box. Let's go grab a nightcap." You knock back a quick one then hightail it home for some well-earned shut-eye. You've extended their good time without letting yours go south.

Drop-ins

Someone shows up uninvited on a Sunday evening, and you just sat down to a book and a plate of Oreos. This is one time when you don't have to be Miss Gracious Hostess. It's called privacy, pal. Sometimes, you got to be alone— recharge the batteries. So when the doorbell rings, don't wig. Grab your purse and coat before answering. Then, make like you were on your way out the door: "Oh gee, I'm sorry. I'm just on my way out. I gotta go take my Aunt Fanny to a Fellini festival. Can I drop you somewhere?"

A TIARA WITH YOUR APRON

Dressing the part

Get in the right mood for playing the hostess with the mostest by climbing out of your business blues. The main idea is the hostess should not just look nice but should stand out from the crowd (so any guest who needs directions to the phone can spot her from across the room). Take advantage. Now's your chance to trot out the getups you wouldn't dare wear on the street: the jewels, the wig, the hostess pajamas, the bright red dress your mother said made you look like a strawberry tart. It's your party. Put on whatever makes you feel comfortable or hot or both. Whatever you wear, put it on before doing your last-minute chores (then at least you'll look ready). The last thing you want is to be tearing up your closet in a fashion crisis while Dick and Jane Early Bird are out in the living room staring at their shoelaces.

KICK OFF YOUR HEELS!

You've mixed cocktails and guests. You've set the mood, the CD player's on rotate. Stop stressing about other people's good time, and let the good time start to find you. The overly solicitous hostess is no better than the neglectful one. She who strives for ease and flair does not badger her guests ("Are you having fun yet?"). At some point, usually about an hour into the wingding, walk out the door then walk back in again. Hang your apron on the coat rack, pretend you don't know all the blood, sweat, and tears that went into this soirée. You're just another lucky guest. Admire the buffet (help yourself to a little something), note how good-looking the crowd is, grab the cutest boy by the elbow and swing.

② Say Thank You

Gratitude and gratuities

Thankfulness and appreciation are the glue of a swell society. Not to mention the grease. There's a time for spreading around the cabbage and a time for laying on the sugar, and a swell always knows what time it is.

TIPPING

Pikers go to the back of the bistro.

Chicks get a bad rap for being chintzy tippers. Let's put an end to that tout de suite. In situations where a gratuity is expected, know how much to give—and then give a little more! When the check arrives, rather than meticulously calculating 15 percent, *round up the figure*, and you'll walk out feeling flush. *Think large*, both in money and in spirit.

To Whom and How Much

Rule of thumb is 15 to 20 percent to everyone. But there are inevitably exceptions and puzzlers—the blowdryer's assistant who went out to get you a coffee? When in doubt, ask at the desk: What's the customary tip?

Hair salons

Twenty percent to the colorist or cutter, and five dollars will get a smile from the shampoo girl. If the magician wielding the bleach wand turns you from mouse to Marilyn, slip an extra ten dollars or so in her envelope, just because she made you feel like a million. If she owns the salon, contrary to the age-old belief, it's no longer uncouth to tip her.

Nail parlor

Twenty percent to the manicurist and pedicurist. After taking care of them, it doesn't hurt to throw five at the boss lady now and then so she'll squeeze you in when you need an emergency touch-up.

Coat check

A buck a coat, two dollars if you're stowing major baggage.

Scuba instructor

The people who add value to your vacation—the skipper, the camel boy, the tour guide—all deserve 15 percent at the end of the excursion. Bump it up to 20 percent if you saw the white gorilla or caught a marlin *this big*.

Skycap or bellman

One to two dollars per bag. Give or take.

Hotel maid

One to three dollars for every day of your stay, left when you check out of the room—the only time she'll find something neatly stacked on your dresser.

Valet parking

One or two dollars when he hands you the keys. If you have to make a quick getaway, give $10 to the attendant to keep your car up front.

Concierge

Doing special favors for the guests is her job, but if she came through with reservations for the hard-to-get-into bistro, you could give her twenty dollars. Some expert wheel-greasers, like Hollywood execs, send flowers to secure good treatment. For those not on an expense account, a thank-you note can't hurt. Even better, make it out to her boss saying how great she is.

Food deliveries

Ten percent of the bill, fifteen if it's raining. Never less than a dollar, even if you only ordered a cup of coffee.

Handymen

Eyeball it. If it's part of his job description, five dollars should cover it. But if he had to lug your air conditioner up three flights of stairs, figure ten dollars for the first ten minutes and five for every fifteen minutes after that. But rarely more than twenty dollars a man.

Blackjack dealer

If you make out big on a hand, say you double down or win a pile on a blackjack, it's nice to push a chip or two in the dealer's direction; he will knock it on the table and slip it in his pocket. And if you're walking away from the table a winner, leave out something for the dealer who brought you luck. Anywhere from five to twenty; but if you're up five hundred bucks, 5 to 10 percent.

Stadium usher

At the ballgame, regular fans hand a coupla bucks to the guy who escorts you to your row. He'll brush the peanut shells off your seat. If you're in the nosebleed section, you can pad the tip, tell him you "forgot your binoculars," and ask if there is anything open further down. Can work at a concert, too.

Shootin' Around

Ilene: Late one night after a Cynthia show, the official party's over and about twenty of us—friends, seamstresses, and firemen-models—aren't ready to call it quits. We go to a little Moroccan den for a celebratory nightcap. Cynthia's still springing. But I figure somebody else ought to pick up the slack—it being her night and all. Unfortunately, Cynthia's got a bad habit of putting up a struggle when anyone tries to treat her. So I wait 'til she's sparked up a conversation with a few of the fireguys, then I catch the barkeep's eye, draw a circle in the air with my finger, and sneak him my plastic. Then when he yells last call and CR reaches into her purse, he tells her, "It's taken care of." Hoodwinked! Nursing our espressos and sambucca, we get to talking about the joys of shooting a round: how we ought to do it more often, and—looking around the room—so should everyone else. It's just one of the many sorely neglected areas of civilized living. There ought to be a book about this stuff, we think. A little looped, we get inspired to write it ourselves.

"Tip," short for "To Insure Promptness," is for anything or anyone. Don't limit it to the usual suspects. Apply the 15 percent rule to all the service people you consider VIP enough for a TIP. The tailor who'll whip out an emergency hem. Give the butcher a bottle of wine now and then. Slip a few bucks to Louie at the fish store who slices your smoked salmon when he hands over your order and you'll get the good stuff he keeps in the back for special customers. Get him used to it and you'll never have to "take a number" again.

DUKING

The green handshake

In a swell world there're two kinds of people: those you tip and those you duke. Tip the cab driver. Duke the doorman who whistled for him. Tip the waiter, duke the person who escorted you to the nice table. Duking is the friendliest form of tipping: cold cash passed in a warm handshake to people who make your life faster, smoother, and friendlier but who never hand you a bill. Strictly off the books, a tip for service beyond the call of duty.

Say you walk into the new joint in town and it's jumping, a terrific state of affairs for all the parties that have a reservation—which yours doesn't. No use wheedling or puffing up into the "Don't you know who I'm gonna be some-

Tipping Back

Bartenders have a code. You should know it. Every third round, a good bartender will rap his knuckles on the bar, signaling, "This one's on the house." Don't revel in the freebie. *Tip back*, whenever you get a bonus drink, dessert, anything. Generally, about half what it would have cost you. More, if you're three sheets to the wind. Or, offer him one on you, not always accepted but invariably appreciated.

day?" routine. Just duke 'em. Little Miss Pinky Ring has the situation under control. Fold a twenty-dollar bill three times, so it's small enough to be cupped in your palm. Then put out your hand (your "duke") and give the maître d' a shake like you mean it. You're asking for a favor, an ace table in a packed room, so make a nice impression. Keep in mind the duker's credo: warm, personal, and discreet. Introduce yourself: *Hi, I'm Pinky. I realize you're awfully busy tonight, and we don't have a reservation, but if there's anything you can do for us we'd appreciate it very much.* Or for a subtler pass, tuck the folded bill between the second and third fingers, then with your arm by your side extend your fingers so the money touches the dukee's hand with either a tap or a push.

Often dukers prefer to express their gratitude on the way out, like if the hostess accommodated your request to relocate from the dog table, between the bus station and the swinging kitchen doors. The exit-duke paves the way for your return. Before long, the bartender will know your "usual" and the maître d' will be greeting you with a smile and a "Right this way!"—straight to the corner booth. Once you're a regular is no time to start taking your friends for granted. Keep on duking. If they try to stop you with a "Fuhgedaboutit," tell them, "It's my pleasure!"

YOUR MONEY'S NO GOOD TONIGHT

Shooting rounds isn't about being a show-off, or just offering an obligatory post-dinner thank-you drink. It's not a quid pro quo thing, keeping tabs on who bought what when. Be a sport, drop a few quid and forget the pro quo. Sometimes it means treating for no reason at all. Maybe you're outnumbered by your guy friends. With them you could probably ride free all night, but why not ratchet up the bonhomie? Be the token girl and one of the boyz by announcing, "First pop's on me." Another scenario: Out on the town with a gaggle of couples, except your girlfriend who's flying solo. When the bill arrives and she has to pay her own way she may feel like a loser. So ride to her side and pony up. "Lulu," you tell her, waving her away as she tries to chip in, "your money's no good tonight."

Go Climb a Tree!

Cynthia: The perfect weekend guest is someone who brings something to do. One time a friend of ours who is a tree surgeon came and brought his harnesses and tree equipment. We climbed trees all weekend in the harnesses, and even put up a tree swing. Another couple once brought binoculars and an identification book for bird-watching. One friend arrived with tarot cards and a for- tune- teller kit. I should have a party where I invite all of them out to the house, then we can predict where the birds'll be and see them up close.

HOUSE CALLS

You never want to greet your hosts empty-handed. And you can't go wrong with wine, flowers, and dessert. But something about presenting a bottle of chardonnay like a passport at a dinner party can seem a little impersonal. The host chirps thanks and has no clue who gave it to her by the time she swallows it. Make your entertaining gifts entertaining, like trashy magazines tied with string and a box of bonbons for a weekend at the beach: "Read it and eat." Going to a Christmas party? Bring a saucer sled, even if the guy lives in an apartment.

Where to get novel visit gifts? Pull them from your own closet's handy-dandy gift shelf, of course. A swell has a bit of the magpie in her, and this is the ideal place to store all the weird stuff that catches your eye on vacation, on the street, or on late-night television, but that you never buy, thinking, *What the heck would I do with it?* Now you know. Spin your random purchase into a visit gift by pairing it with something useful or at least funny.

Kooky Kollectible	Saving Spin
Cheap sombrero from Tijuana	Filled with lemons and a bottle of tequila
Box of good luck charms: a horseshoe, silver wishbones, etc.	Tied around the bottle of wine for a bon-voyage dinner or other "Mazel tov" event
Pair of baby-size beaded slippers picked up in Istanbul	With a copy of *Aladdin* when visiting pals with a new tot
A Veg-O-Matic (slices, dices, even juliennes)	And a grocery bag of crudité fixings
Stack of sale-priced Cary Grant movies	Held together with a black bow-tie
Box of Mr. Bubble	With a bottle of bubbly

Thank-You-Grams

Just write 'em, immediately and for all occasions, on all kinds of stationery: postcards, the back of a photo, whatever it takes to get 'em out fast. Best the day after. Don't go more than a week, but better belated than never. Keep school supplies on hand: stamps, envelopes, tape, glue, box of three-by-five cards imprinted with your name. For added zip, stuff a post-party favor in the envelope: a candy bar from your bag and a note: *So sweet of you to have us over.* Or a balloon *on which you've written in magic marker, What a blowout!*

How to arrive empty-handed

With a Polaroid camera and a ribbon. At the end of the night, take the camera, leave the photos, tied up with a bow—a g'bye gift.

Love

Go ahead and take a gamble.
So what if you lose your shirt?

L ove's a crapshoot, baby. You don't always hit seven on your first roll. Sure, everyone wants to walk away a winner, with a lifetime supply of a cutie called Chip. But you can't only measure a romance by the final payout. There are plenty of kicks to be had along the way, from the first flirt to the ring-a-ding fling of a lifetime. And keep in mind that a good gambler doesn't sweat every hand. Worrying why last night's Mr. Right hasn't called? Did I talk too much? Should I not have slept over so soon? Now hear this: There are no fool-proof systems. So what if Last-minute Larry just showed up at your door Saturday night. If you're free, take him for a spin. Drop the lasso. Not every affair ends up at the Elvis Chapel, but that doesn't mean it wasn't worth the trip to Vegas.

THE FELONIOUS FLIRT

How come a flirty chick always comes off like some goo-goo-eyed ditz, but a flirty guy gets a rep as an intriguing rogue, an irresistible rapscallion, as if he's some kind of fascinating criminal? Well, if flirting's a crime, then a swell girl should plead *guilty as charged*. That's not a high sign to start hatching elaborate plots and maneuvers. You're not committing a jewel heist. Think more like a grifter working off the cuff. Flirting is a confidence game and everyone's a fair mark.

When Babyface Betty, wanted for flirting with reckless abandon, is on a spree, she's spreading around the charms like freshly minted C-notes. "Hiya, handsome!" she calls to the doorman, still rubbing the sleep outta her eyes. To get a chortle out of a fellow sardine on the subway, she knocks on his newspaper and asks, "Excuse me, sir. Is this first class?" At a hot spot, BB robs the coat-check girl of her snippy attitude by tossing her a compliment on her lipstick.

Easy as pie when the stakes are small. But what about when you're at a party and find yourself eye-to-chest with Heavenly Harry and there's steam in the air? Don't change a thing. Resist the temptation to fall back on safe-and-effective flirting techniques: wide-eyed smile, coy arm touch, mirrored body language, not letting yourself be "too funny." C'mon, there're more ways than that to skin a tomcat.

So go ahead and tell your jury-duty story without worrying if it's too long or crazy. Be your own screwy, enthusiastic self. If you're bored with giving your vital statistics for the tenth time that night, invent an outlandish biography—you can come clean later. When the conversation is speeding along and you notice his drink is below empty, offer to fetch a refill. En route to the bar, run behind the couch and do your "mime descending a staircase." So what if it's a terrible comedy routine? Flirting is a victimless crime. You're in this racket for your own amusement

> ## Going Down?
>
> **Ilene:** *Cynthia and I are minding our own business in the elevator when she announces that her tights are in a twist, only she can't fix them on account of the gray-flanneled stranger on board. Then Cynthia stops fidgeting and with all the sweet charm of a mobster's moll asks the suit, "Excuse me, but would you mind turning around for a minute?" I make a little circle with my index finger, the international hand signal for Face the wall, Bub. And to my surprise, he does. "No peeking," I say, while Cynthia lifts her skirt and corrects the situation. Dinging at the lobby, the doors open and he, all sheepish and courtly, waves us ahead. We got a kinky frisson from this brief unscheduled encounter. And judging by the flush in Mr. Gray Flannel's cheeks, going down those nineteen floors gave him a lift, too.*

as much as for any material or matrimonial gain. If you end up in the getaway cab with a big score, whoopee!

CUT TO THE CHASE

Think of love as an action flick, not a five-hanky weeper. It's filled with chemical explosions, suspense, and, of course, great chase scenes. The most exciting movies keep you guessing for the first twenty minutes. Translate that to your off-screen intrigues. Not being sure how you feel about him (and vice versa) is no reason to walk out of the theater. If the action grabs you, go with it. Whether he's on your tail, or you're heading the wrong way down a one-way street after him, make scenes memorable, packed with bold responses, surprising twists, some innocent subterfuge, and spontaneous invitations.

BEDSIDE MANNERS

Even the all-time great affairs are filled with awkward moments: the first doorway "G'nite," the transition to

"I'd like to thank the Academy"

Cynthia: The second time my hubby and I met he thought it was the first. The bum didn't remember me. I'd been looking forward to seeing him again at our friend's birthday blast for weeks. I'd even marked in my calendar, "Wear something good." He was just how I remembered him at the party three years ago, except for the sexpot flypapered to him. When he hit the buffet, I saw my opening. I cozied up next to him on the couch with my plate loaded high, so I'd have to be there for a while. The flygirl had to go stick on someone else. We hit it off. The last to leave, we were the lingerers helping the host out with the dishes. But he still hadn't asked for my number, and almost all the glasses were dry. I had to find a way to give him my 411—and an incentive to call. I invited him to my annual Academy Awards party Monday night (my first annual, but he didn't have to know that). If ever I needed a reason to throw a party, he was standing right in front of me. So I'd have to find guests on two days' notice. He'd be worth it—if he'd show up. He did, and was the only guy theme-dressed in a tux. When the rest of the guests had gone and he rolled up his French cuffs to help wash the dishes, I had a feeling he might stay in the picture.

separate-but-equal toothbrushes. The tendency is to overdiagnose these romantic growing pains—a waste of time since you're never going to know exactly what to do (and your girlfriends won't either). In the first blush of love, follow the physician's prime directive: *Do no harm*. Don't perform unnecessary surgery on a relationship that wasn't sick in the first place. And keep the spirits up even in potentially fatal scenes. Here, a few textbook examples.

You're pillow-talking, he's in a coma.

Hitting the hay is no time to get deep. It's been a long day—and night! The last thing you want is him nodding off in the middle of your account of your parents' second divorce. You're nose-to-nose, just having done the dirty deed, the urge is to share. So talk about your scars. *Not* a detailed account of the wounds inflicted by your last bastardly beau. Show him the stitches on your knee you got table-dancing in Acapulco, the burn welt from when you were a Campfire Girl. Intimate moments don't have to be heavy. You'll both sleep better if you conk out on a laugh rather than on an issue-stained pillowcase.

The morning after: Scram or scramble eggs?

You wake up next to a two hundred twenty-pound dumbbell named Snoring Bob. After staring at the ceiling for what feels like hours, it's still too early for a believable excuse to hit the road. Set the clock ahead two hours and feign panic: "Omigod, it's ten o'clock. Gotta get to work." Then *run away*. But if you open your eyes and after one glimpse think you're still dreaming, figure out a way to make Sunday last all day long. Not by asking meekly, "What are you doing today?" (Puts him on the spot.) Be cling-free like fabric softener. Tell him what *you've* got in store: "I'm going to the Museum of TV and Radio to watch some classic *Mission Impossible* episodes." If he looks interested, tell him to grab his hat, 'cause in five minutes the invitation will self-destruct.

The sweetie called you at work to say "I miss you," and busy you bit his head off.

By all means tell him your boss is a nightmare and your assistant ate your homework. But an explanation without contrition is just rationalization. "I'm stressed" is not an apology. "I'm sorry" is. Those two words cannot be overvalued. They don't cost a dime, but they buy a lot of good will.

The no-pajama party was Saturday. No word on Sunday.

What are you gonna do, call your lawyer? Before you slept over, did he sign anything promising to respond within twenty-four hours? You have no case. *Should I call him?* Flip a coin. Better yet, avoid the waiting altogether with the underutilized next day "Thanks for everything" phone call. And his feelings, whatever they may be, won't be changed either way.

You're sprinting home to let him in—again.

Not every big step has to be a big talkfest. If you're ready for a key exchange, make it a casual occasion, not a somber ceremony. When you go to the key place for a copy, ask them for one of those hotel-room attachments, ideally with your apartment number stamped on it. Then when he's leaving one morning, hide it in his pocket with a note: "Check in any time."

The lout said seven o'clock, now it's the bottom of the hour and your second martini.

If the bar he's kept you waiting in is in America, he's innocent until proven guilty. Look at it this way: He's probably sweating every traffic light worried that you're steamed. Meanwhile, how often do your thoughts get a half hour to themselves? You're sitting pretty! When he straggles in, don't put on your sour puss and bark, "You're late!" Give him a chance to tell you what held him up. And if it turns out he was lingering over bevvies with the boys, you'll get your chance to make him pay for it—*when you open the wine list.*

He's perfect, except for that jean jacket with the dragon on the back.

Like the song from *Guys and Dolls* says, "Every time a girl finds a guy who fits, she

---

Meeting Madame Ex

Ilene: *There's no greater challenge to a girl's gallant side than an unscheduled encounter with his ex. Once when I was accompanying my guy to a function in his hometown, amid his friends and family, I had the dubious pleasure of noticing a striking glamazon making a beeline for my boy. Wouldn't you know she was Madame Ex. Even after he introduced me as his girlfriend, she still tried to respark their old flame. Right in front of me! She hectored him for not being in touch, berated him to see her next time she's in the city. When she had the nerve to demand his number, I didn't slug her. I produced his business card from my purse and handed it over with a calm smile. A good move, and I wish I could say I planned it. Still, she saw my hands weren't shaking and got the point: Go ahead, call all you like. I'm not worried, because he's mine.*

takes him in for alterations." You don't want to totally change him, but everyone can use some fine-tuning. Maybe the problem isn't that your boyfriend is an accountant, it's that he dresses like one. Loosen or spiff him up as needed, but slowly. To make his nerd look read cooler, pick him up a pair of Elvis Costello glasses. Even the most hard-case slob or square has an inner fashion fantasy life. Help him tap into it. If you suspect your lumberjack would look, and feel, sexier in sweaters, bring home a Steve McQueen movie and drop a few hints. "Is it me, or are those turtlenecks making me hot?"

CHIVALRY

It isn't totally dead, but when was the last time a guy stood up when you walked into a room? Gal gallante to the rescue, filling the chivalry vacuum with any chance to perform an act of courtesy, generosity, or courage. If he doesn't open the door for you, maybe he's just not a door-opening kind of guy. Hold it for *him*. Spring for him now and then, whether he's a big spender, gets short arms when the bill arrives—or even if you're in the habit of going Dutch. To avoid an unseemly tug-of-war, give the waiter your plastic en route to the powder room.

But gallantry is about more than money and doorways. Be his champion, his damsel in shining armor. If everyone's making fun of his new haircut, rather than chime in with "His barber cuts with a lawn mower," be the lone voice to claim the shag cute. Let no one sully the name of the man you love. When legendary agent Irving "Swifty" Lazar married at age fifty-three, his wife Mary thought the lifelong nickname sounded demeaning, so she always called him Irving. Soon she had everyone calling him that, too—at least to his face.

Go out of your way to extend yourself for the ladies, as well as your man. Notice the invisible girl staring into her Clamato at a noisy brunch and steer the conversation her way. Don't leave her hanging just because she's a dish. The hotter she is, the better you'll look for being her Princess Valiant.

Miss Saturday Night

Whether you've been dating five days or married five years, you can always ask your heartthrob if he's free on Saturday night. Let's assume you've both had your fill of precious bed-and-breakfasts, international coffee commercial moments, and fancy French bistros. Your big night on the town can be a foray to the corner biker bar you'd never dare try; or make him an invitation to a picnic and roll-in-the-grass in your backyard. The antidate can be the antidote to relationship ennui.

I Gave at the Office

Ilene: Poor guy, out of town on business for his birthday. He said he didn't care, but I knew he'd be blue. Even if I wouldn't be out there until the weekend, I could still help him ring in the big day by ringing up a few long-distance surprises. First I hired Lucille the masseuse, the next best thing to me in the flesh, to make a house call to his hotel room in the morning. Then, the local bakery arrived with a baby chocolate birthday cake covered with flowers and a candle. And finally a promising delivery from Frederick's of Hollywood: a naughty nothing with black maribou trim for me, and a snakeskin banana hammock for him. Just in case he and Lucille got the wrong idea, I included a note: *Save for Sunday!*

Naked Saturday

Put on your pair of fuzzy slippers and you're both dressed for the day. Makes chores more stimulating. Fold the laundry, putting the dryer lint in your belly-button (it's clean!) and have him take it out.

Home videos

Skip the popcorn and porn—too obvious. Try another take: Japanese Horror Night. Serve cold sushi and hot sake. Slip in and out of your kimono, geisha-style. And when you cry "Oh, Godzilla!" move your lips a few seconds before letting out sound.

Check into Motel Sex

When looking for an idyllic getaway, you don't have to drive five hours to Quaintsville, U.S.A. Just pull off the interstate. There's nothing sexier than an anonymous motel room stocked with all the necessities for an illicit rendezvous. Magic fingers! Fifty-eight channels. OK, so no mountains to hike. Naked relays to the ice machine burn calories, too.

Go on the lam

For the price of a night at the multiplex, buy your own Hollywood getaway scene. Instruct him to meet you at the train station. Pretend you've been spotted and have to get outta town on the double. Ask the clerk for two tix on the next train and hurry on board looking suspicious. After a few stops, when the coast seems clear, get off. Check out the town, see if it's a good place to start life over, or at least get a burger.

Mystery night

One week he surprises you with opera tickets. Next time, you take him out—to a Little League game. Trade off. A bird tour of the park, a day at the races, dinner at the skating rink, all the sangria you can drink hopping tapas bars. Out of ideas? Blindfold him, drive around the block, and bring him back home.

Poetry for the Ferklempt

My heart swells / So I must tell / The whole world / How I . . . (consult rhyming dictionary) . . . *hurled*, trying to compose your gushing self in a sonnet for sweetie. If you're overwhelmed with verse-worthy feelings, and words fail you—not to mention rhyme, simile, and metaphor—despair not. Give it a shot. Poetry comes in many forms. Minimize the words, and think up new mediums for your message. A few brief words in laundry marker on a pair of his neatly folded briefs. Sidewalk chalk in front of his apartment building. A book of embarrassing love poems that keep turning up under his cereal bowl, in his desk, under his pillow. A telegram with an urgent message to report for active duty at your place at 0800 hours.

Good Things Come in Weird Packages

"It's the thought that counts."

This usually means the gift rotted. Maybe the giver wasn't doing the right kind of thinking. A truly thoughtful gift starts with an observation. He loves his cats: Plant his backyard with catnip and watch the kitties go kookoo. He made the best apple sauce you ever tasted: Give him an apple corer, and while you're at it, an apple tree bearing the note, "Don't sit under with anyone but me."

Let little ideas mushroom.

You've noticed that every time he's handed a wine list, he turns redder than the merlot. Give him a pocket primer, and throw in a wine appreciation course—for two. Not all gifts should be corrective though. Indulge his passions *and* his weaknesses. If he's a sofa spud, rather than buy theater tickets, get him a cozy afghan and a coupla videos—one naughty, one nice.

As the calendar pages blow toward V-Day, you're thumbing through catalogs, deliberating between a singing umbrella (would he find it funny?) and an electric loofah (would he use it?). Red alert! Jump out of your mental tie box. Sure, you don't want to be the fourth girlfriend to give him boxers with hearts, but you can re-release the classics. Give him a box of chocolates—a big red toolbox loaded with red-handled screwdrivers, a hammer, a power drill, and sweetened with Hershey's kisses. (With all those drill bits and screws, you should have no trouble thinking of a sexy note.) Try a panty bouquet: Roll up a dozen red lacey undies in a box full of long-stems. Apply the same fuzzy logic to every gifting opportunity.

Care packages

Come through when it counts. Whether it's his birthday or a sick day, if you can't be by his side, get on the phone. But don't dial his number yet. Your voice is great, but how about something tangible? When he's home with a 102-degree fever, warm words don't cut it, he needs hot soup. Get the neighborhood deli to make a chicken noodle delivery.

OVER EASY

In the middle ages, it was customary to tip the executioner to ensure that he would sharpen his ax before delivering the fatal blow. They valued a clean break. So should you. Face the music. *Bon courage!*

The Kiss Off

Maybe his only crime was making you fall asleep over your mashed potatoes. Or perhaps you found your best friend's Wonderbra in his sock drawer. Either way, he's getting the heave-ho. And either way, you shouldn't have to sputter a bunch of guilty mumbo jumbo about how you're not over your last boyfriend, or how you're about to be put on medication for your chronic commitment-phobia. A long-term situation may require serious break-up negotiations. But if he's a short-timer and already you'd rather get a bikini wax than catch a flick with him, a "major talk" is not required. Just beg off with a "Sorry. I can't. But thanks." If you feel you got more 'splaining to do, detailing his flaws isn't going to make either of you feel better. Focus on the good stuff, even as you say goodbye. Flatter him out the door. "Jerry, I had a great time at the monster truck rally. Hilarious. I'll never forget it. But about Tues . . . I can't . . . I know, and you're a helluva sweetheart for taking me to *Riverdance*. And that karaoke bar. Crazy! OK. You're the greatest. No, you're great. OK, bye!"

Happy Wallow-Days

So your dreamboat throws you overboard without a life preserver. You'll live. But not right away. As with a hangover, the best salve for a broken heart is to surrender to the pain and misery. Trying to look on the bright side too soon is gonna give you a blinding headache. There is a time for darkness, and this is it. Forget blind dates, just lower the blinds. Here are a few suggestions on how to make the most of your wallow days.

Refeather your nest

You're going through emotional highs and lows. Soften the landings. Redecorate later. For now, take to your bed and convalesce in style. Paint your pout and prop yourself up on your shag rug, with pillows, Kleenex, maribou slippers, Mallomars—and cry your eyes out in the arms of your bubbly best friend, Miss Veuve Cliquot. Then dial all your friends, tell them you're going to "end it all." Let them remind you of all the things you have to live for. Whatever you do, don't call *him* and ask *why*. (He doesn't know.) Enjoy your own miserable company. Lounge around in a filthy slip, popping bonbons into your mouth in front of *The Way We Were*, or whatever gets your self-pity juices flowing.

Take a cruise

In the old days, when a nice girl suffered a tragic romantic setback, her family would send her away on a long cruise in the hope that she would get distracted and forget all about the brute. So civilized! It can work for you. Rent a motorcycle or a convertible, wrap a scarf around your head, and drive somewhere you've never been. Find a restaurant with a light in the window, tell the owner your sad story. Check out for a while and into a motel, live on Ho-Hos, hooch, and call-in radio programs. Maybe someone out there on the air will understand. Toy with the idea of having your own show on the Food Network.

The Big-Bang Theory

Get it all out of your system at once. When the friends insist on dragging you out of the abyss, you can't resist forever. Don't let them haul your sorry butt to a step class. Tell them to throw you a bachelorette party—at the pistol range. The targets are silhouettes of Mr. Wrong. Watch men pound each other senseless at a prizefight. Or relive the crash and burn, this time cheering, at the demolition derby. Enjoy!

DATING THROUGH DRY SPELLS

In between boyfriends, the pressure's on either to "get back out there" or "be okay on your own." But there's another way to cross the desert en route to your next romantic oasis. Rustle up a few sherpas—the fellas who are happy to keep your canteen full and point out the sights. In the old days they called the guys who escort you out on the town "walkers"—dates with no strings attached.

My Year of Dating Dangerously

Ilene: They called me LGB, the Last Great Broad. That's because I didn't care if they were married, just in from out of town for a few nights, or an ex-someone from my past. For an evening of platonic entertainment, I was very available. When Bill Z. would come in from Chicago, he knew he could count on me to fill the empty seat at dinner. Chris could ring at 5 o'clock and I'd stand in for the chippie who canceled. With me they knew they didn't have to worry about offending by calling last minute, answering questions about where things were going to lead, or who else was going to tag along. I was just along for the ride—ready and willing for some innocent action. The irony was that they treated me like gold, showing courtly manners I never knew they had in them, offering me the plum Knicks ticket and buying me all the beer and dogs I could eat.

I was in a zone. One night, I was at a party at Elaine's with a handsome fella named Rick. While at the bar, David H., another one of my platonic steadies, asked him, "So, are you her walker tonight?" Rick didn't take kindly to the label and said indeed he was not. Little did I know, that night, he vowed not to be mistaken for just another stag. It took six months of friendly "dating" before I realized my feelings for him weren't so innocent either. I'd started out embracing the abyss, and ended up kissing the sherpa.

HAPPILY EVER AFTER

So you shoot seven and wind up marching down the aisle with Mr. Lucky. Now what? The threshold isn't the finish line. Keep on fanning the flames. "Husbands are like a fire; they go out when unattended," said Zsa Zsa Gabor, who married eight times, but never gave up on the institution. In other words, don't take him for granted. Remember how hard he was to find. And, keep his dice hot.

④ Get Around

A top-down girl in a hard-top world

As theater critics and restaurant reviewers remind us, destinations are often overrated. A swell knows not to ignore the action in the journey.

DASHING

You know how to whistle for a taxi, don't you?

Waving and hailing are fine and well, but when you need to capture a cabbie's attention, whistle, four-finger style: With both hands, index and middle fingers touching, form a V. Stretch lips really taut and curled over teeth, then jut your jaw out. With four fingertips touch the tip of your tongue and push it back, leaving a space between the bottom lip and your two middle fingers. (That's the only place where air should escape.) Then blow. Takes practice.

Climb into a jeep without flashing panty

Whether it's the paparazzi or a bunch of construction workers watching, a lady doesn't cause a commotion. Take a note from the glitterati, who know how to make an exit, showing maximum leg and minimum knickers. In a pencil skirt, or a micro mini, back into the vehicle, legs together until you hit the seat, then swing them in after you. To alight, edge your bottom to the end of the seat, drop your purse, brace yourself with your hands, then swivel. Once your gams are out, push off. That way, even if someone offers a hand of assistance, you appear to spring forth with weightless grace.

Pumps attract trouble. You better know how to run in them. When the train's pulling out of the station, make like Angie Dickinson—Pepper in *Police Woman*—weight on the toes and make those wheels fly. That was Ginger Rogers's trick, too. You'd never catch her at a wedding chucking her shoes to dance in bare feet.

DRIVE-THRU PARTY

A party can be like a prison. Getting in's easy. Getting out's the hard part, especially if you're on a time budget. The art of making an appearance—for maximum exposure and fun—is worth mastering. A page ripped from the Diary of a Mad Partygoer:

Drop coat. Beeline for hostess. Don't want to get pinned in a corner before punching in. Quick "Hi." Hate it when people say "can't stay" the minute they walk in the door. Must sample as many snacks and guests as possible. Oh, there's Griffin. Nice talking to him again, but gotta keep moving. Employ double-entendre trick. When he says he didn't make much up front on the deal but hopes to get something in *the back end*, tell him he's got a dirty mind and make tracks. Get derailed by discussion of Polish cinema. Attention drifts to glistening pile of chicken. Catch Simone as she passes and employ rope-in-a-friend trick. Head for the poultry. Lewis and Guy are fighting, want to know once and for all, who's a worse flirt. Emergency! Use last escape option: the fake sneeze followed by the international sign for "Need a Kleenex." Yikes, nine o'clock! Find Hilly. "Loved meeting the cute boyfriend." Specific compliments are best. "So early!" she begs. (Hostess abandonment issues.) Be reassuring. "I had such a good time"—reach into pocket and pull out purloined pistachio nuts—"I took souvenirs." Laugh when she offers you a couple of buffalo wings, too. Kiss g'bye and hit the road.

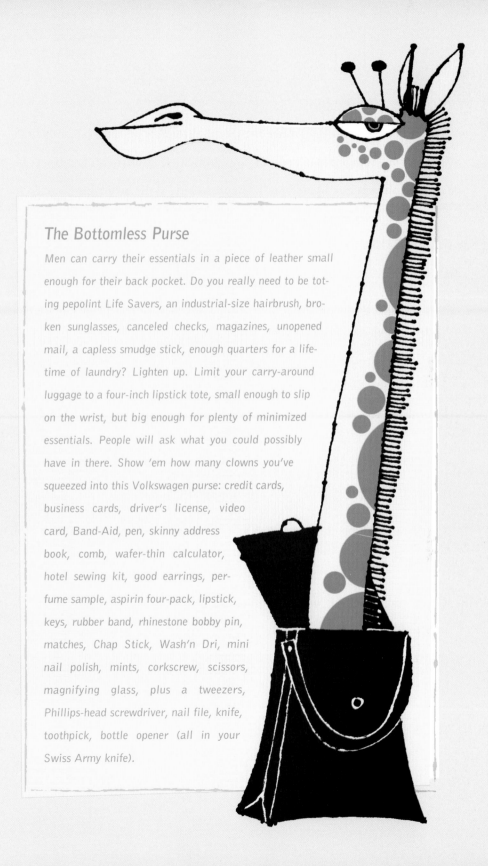

The Bottomless Purse

Men can carry their essentials in a piece of leather small enough for their back pocket. Do you really need to be toting pepolint Life Savers, an industrial-size hairbrush, broken sunglasses, canceled checks, magazines, unopened mail, a capless smudge stick, enough quarters for a lifetime of laundry? Lighten up. Limit your carry-around luggage to a four-inch lipstick tote, small enough to slip on the wrist, but big enough for plenty of minimized essentials. People will ask what you could possibly have in there. Show 'em how many clowns you've squeezed into this Volkswagen purse: credit cards, business cards, driver's license, video card, Band-Aid, pen, skinny address book, comb, wafer-thin calculator, hotel sewing kit, good earrings, perfume sample, aspirin four-pack, lipstick, keys, rubber band, rhinestone bobby pin, matches, Chap Stick, Wash'n Dri, mini nail polish, mints, corkscrew, scissors, magnifying glass, plus a tweezers, Phillips-head screwdriver, nail file, knife, toothpick, bottle opener (all in your Swiss Army knife).

EARLY BIRDS ARE SPECIAL

A swell understands the difference between fashionably late and late. It's OK to arrive at the eleventh hour of a big wingding to revive the embers of a fading crowd. But when it's personal, a friend waiting alone at the bar, a roast in the oven, or a ferry everyone's catching, a swell is prompt! Then it isn't stylish to oversleep or have a fashion crisis, even if it means faking yourself out, setting your watch fifteen minutes fast to be *on time*. But in an emergency (like when you oversleep or have a fashion crisis), break safety glass containing these five desperate excuses for being late.

1. I was working on a surprise for you. I can't tell you what it is, but I think you're really gonna like it.

2. Something really great happened. I can't say or I'll jinx it. But believe me, if it works out, you're golden.

3. Carry a prewritten note, excusing your lateness, written and signed, "The Cab Driver."

4. Claim you thought it was . . . something that rhymes. If the dinner's at Mitali's, tell 'em you thought they said Vitale's and have been all over Little Italy looking for it.

5. I was baking you those cookies you love, and I set off the smoke alarm in my apartment.

STOP AND SMELL THE LANDFILL

Don't let this happen to you:

Friend: "Can you believe they're tearing down that cool old Bob's Big Boy franchise from the fifties?"

You: "Huh?"

Friend: "You know, on Route 27, right near your office. You must go by it twice a day."

You: "Oh, I never noticed it."

Commuting to work, you're on mental cruise control. Even trips filled with green become a gray blur. The only thing that changes is which side the sun's on. But this trek may be the only one you can take for a week. Treat it like the excursion you can't afford to go on for another three months. So Tuscany's got to wait. Imagine you're on the Via Veneto, switching off your morning radio show, plugging in Italian language tapes while wearing all your gold jewelry and sipping a cappuccino. Start daytripping: Wake up early and take the long cut. See the sights: Stop at the park you always pass and feed the squirrels. Skip the gym and power bar for a bucket of balls at the driving range. Try a new mode of transportation. Get out from underground and go the whole sixty blocks on foot, bring your binoculars to check out the tops of the buildings. Rent a convertible or a pickup truck for a week. Experiment with non-work commutes, too. Coming home in the wee hours, sex siren Ava Gardner was known to hitch a ride on a garbage truck, still in her evening gown. Then again, this was a woman who skied through shark-infested waters to the set of *Night of the Iguana* while the rest of the cast took a boat.

TOURIST TRAPS

Before your next trip, imagine you have to write a "What I Did on My Two-Week Vacation" essay. Do you really want to say, "I saw lots of old cherchs that were Old and a hotle. It wuz neat"? The cute, out-of-the-way raw bar and the tree-swinging adventure in a Costa Rican inn are "charming and undiscovered"—except by all the other tourists who bought the same "Let's Go Offbeat" book you did. Come up with your own package tours, historic sites, ideas of extreme fun. A few itinerant itineraries:

Outward bound or bust

With a sidekick, hit the road and see how much mileage you can get out of a gas card and one hundred dollars in cash each. Live off the land: Scout for happy hours with the best free grub; tune in to local radio stations announcing joints where "ladies drink free." Hit art galleries at closing time, in case anyone's having a wine-and-cheese.

Grandma's Big Blast

Cynthia: I didn't plan it as a family vacation. It just happened that way. At breakfast, I'm looking through the newspaper for getaway inspiration (good as any guide book), when I spot a story about the shuttle launch. Hmm, Cape Canaveral. I call NASA and get the launch schedule. One of the dates just so happens to be Grandma's birthday. Instead of ruling that day out, I give Grandma a ring and invite her along. Then, the rest of the family wants in, too. Suddenly, it's my childhood all over again. Everyone flies to Miami and we rent a Winnebago, load it up with birthday trimmings: cake, champagne, caviar. We drive four hours, arriving just in time for the one A.M. launch—to be delayed. We wait, standing on the beach in the middle of the night, buying coffees every five minutes, ice creams, souvenirs, taking turns napping. All of us except Grandma, that is, who stands vigil wide awake until four A.M. when the rocket finally blasts off. She says only one word: "Awesome."

Meat Me in Amarillo

Ilene: Benny (my college sweetheart) and I are off on a spring-break cross-country dash to deliver a friend's car to San Diego. An hour on the road and he leaves his wallet at a HoJo's phone booth on the New Jersey Turnpike. This we discover when the bacon stops us for speeding. Benny's caught without his license and the car is registered in his friend's name. Looks like he's spending the night in the big house. So I fake an asthma attack 'til the fuzz gets exhausted and lets us go.

No dough, no license, no plastic. Either we call our parents shamefaced, or we make a run for it on the three hundred dollars in my pocket. We run, eating baloney and crashing in campgrounds after dark. When we get to Amarillo, Texas, we see a banner advertising a "free 72-ounce steak dinner" for anyone who can finish a four-pound slab of beef; plus potato, shrimp, and all the fixings; in an hour—without upchucking. The catch: Losers have to cough up $48.50. That would leave us $7.50 to get to San Diego. But Benny has been eating canned beans for days. He is desperate. In the first ten minutes, he plows through half the beast. I cheer, "All right! No problem." He shakes his head: "Can't eat anymore." I'm like, "Whaddyamean?" Spotting one of the fringe-skirted cowgirls patrolling the joint, I tell him, "Quick, throw me that piece." I catch a hunk under the table and drop it into my Timberland. He tosses me another that I swallow whole. So much for being a vegetarian. Before long, the cowbell rings and an announcer calls out, "Ladies and gentlemen, we'd like to announce a new member of the 72-Ounce Steak Club! Señor Benny! Come on up here and bring your purdy wife too!" Luckily no one hears the meat squishing in my shoes.

Enough with the wine country!

A girl can only drink so much chardonnay. There's plenty of other scenic tastings to seek out. Try the hometown of your favorite candy bar; the Sugar Bush in Minnesota, where they make maple syrup and let you sample boiling sap on sticks; Brooklyn's famous Gold's Horseradish factory; the Pez dispensary in Orange, Connecticut; a barbecue shack tour of Charles County, Maryland.

Voyage back in time

Shecky Green was your late uncle Al's favorite comedian. You discover the old yuckster hasn't gone to the big dressing room in the sky but is alive and well and still working the retirement belt. As a tribute to Al, catch Shecky's shtick before it's too late. Relive the jokes that cracked you up when you were twelve. Make it the first leg of your Where Are They Now? Legend Series. Next stop: Eartha Kitt at the Carlyle, Wayne Newton in Vegas.

Wonders of the world

Set a lifetime goal, like seeing all the Wonders, the seven ancient, seven modern, seven natural. That's twenty-two in all, if you count Stevie.

AIRPORT ANXIETY

Traveling brings out people's inner refugee. They dress like slobs, take everything they own, cramming the excess into shopping-bag carry-ons. . . . What happened to the days when flying was considered a first-class journey, no matter where you were sitting on the plane? Back when commercial air travel was still new and cool, arrivals and departures were glamorous scenes filled with mystery and possibility: strangers on a plane, stewardesses in Pucci uniforms. Women wore travel suits and called a suitcase a valise. So lose the Ellis Island luggage and start moving in style.

Leave the track suit at home

Spiff up for the airport and you feel ready for adventure, and any chance encounter. Why buy another lizard handbag but keep the fraying nylon shlep sack? Invest in a nice piece or two. If you look like class, casually chic, you're more likely to get bumped up to a better one—from Coach to Business or First. Hotels notice, too, if you look Ritzy and pack well.

Valise vivisection

Heavy stuff on bottom: shoes, books, tennis racket, blow dryer, cosmetics (in a small waterproof bag, so if something leaks it won't spill over everything). Next: underwear, swimsuits, T-shirts, jeans, things that don't wrinkle. Then, for the fragile layers, the dry-cleaner plastic trick: Hang the garment in plastic, fold it, then take out the hanger. As soon as you get where you're going (even before checking the minibar), hang up the top layer in the shower, where you can steam it (in the plastic to avoid water damage).

Less is less

Wise fortune cookie say, "She who can stow her baggage in the overhead compartment never has to visit the Lost and Found." Baggage is a metaphor: Don't pack more than you can carry. Keep a cosmetic kit in the closet with miniature duplicates of your staples. To leave room for acquisitions, pare down shoes to sneakers or comfy flats, one pair of heels (sandals in summer). Repeat outfits. Changing clothes every day is an American obsession. Think like a broad abroad, even if you're only on the way to San Jose. Ask any guy what he finds more attractive: a girl wearing the same black dress in three different cities, or the one who makes him tie and untie the rent-a-car trunk to fit a suitcase filled with her hair products.

RIDING SHOTGUN

In Bonnie and Clyde's day someone had to be on guard. The passenger seat is upholstered with responsibilities beyond chipping in for tolls and gas.

Navigation: the orderly folding and decoding of maps; the willingness to jump out at a red light and ask for directions (or flag down the coppers if the situation's getting desperate—it might get you your own personal police motorcade). Keep a pad and pen to write down directions so you don't end up like a bad comedy routine: "I thought *you* were listening!"

Mental support: Don't conk out. But you're not staying awake to front-seat drive, huffing over a missed exit. You'll get there eventually. Meanwhile, you're having fun because you brought your diary to read aloud, a greatest hits tape of your stupidest answering machine messages, not to mention a glove compartment stash of snacks, a harmonica, sunscreen, a hat, mints, and a poetry book to soothe the savage gridlocked breast.

Grease Monkey Business

Car trouble! You pull onto the shoulder. Two options: Hike up your skirt and turn on the flashers in hopes that a passerby will take pity on you; or get some grease under your nails and fix it yourself like a real woman! We can't give you the whole garage, just a couple of tips that might jumper-cable you through a breakdown.

Overheating

When it's 102 degrees out and there's steam curling up from under the hood, look at the temperature gauge. If it's on H (hot), turn off the A/C and open the windows. If that doesn't bring the needle down, take off your shirt and turn *on* the heat. This allows coolant to circulate through the engine. If you're stuck in traffic, avoid the problem by not letting the engine idle. Put the car in neutral and depress the accelerator lightly to keep the fans going and the engine cool. If none of that works, you're going to have to pull your water bottle from your gym bag and dump it in the radiator. Pull into the shade, open the hood, and wait at least twenty minutes. Then find the thing that looks like an attaché case with a cap, take a rag and hold it over the cap, press down hard, and unscrew counterclockwise SLOWLY (so it doesn't explode).

A flat

This is for when the guy in the red Jag you're chasing throws a box of tacks out the window. Roll the car somewhere as flat as your tire. Hood up, hazards on. You'll need the jack, spare, and other standard flat-changing hardware. But what they don't pack in the trunk that every lug wench worth her weight in Valvoline keeps in there too is a blanket to stick between your new slacks and the gravel, a pair of heavy gloves, and a couple of plastic newspaper delivery bags (ends cut off and they pull on as antigrease sleeve protectors). Where to put the jack is posted on the lid of the trunk. Put a big rock or a wedge behind the wheel diagonal to the flat so the car doesn't roll away. Raise the car two to three inches above the ground, work your magic with the lug wrench, and you've done it! Now the hard part, putting everything back. It's like putting toothpaste back in the tube. The obsessive-compulsive greaser keeps a Polaroid of the pre-unpacked jack to know where everything goes.

Snowed in

Ski trip, seven A.M. Powder! You're about to hit the slopes, but where's the car? After you've dug up the buried vehicle, the door's frozen shut. Your blow dryer (and a lot of extension cord) can solve the problem. If the lock's stuck and your Conair isn't around, heat the key up with a flick of your Bic. Works on carburetors, too.

Let's Get Lost

The road to hell is paved with good intentions. So's the one you've been driving back and forth on for the last hour searching for exit 57K. When the outdoor concert you had tickets for is way past intermission and the highway still looks like a Roadrunner cartoon, the moment has come to tie a white handkerchief to the antenna and surrender. You're lost. Accept that the show will go on without you. Let all that tension and guilt evaporate. Embrace the freedom of being an accidental tourist. Turn to the passenger seat and say, "At least there's two of us." (Hopefully there's someone in the passenger seat when you say this.) Then explore the mysterious land where you've landed. That's how some of the best discoveries were made—from Columbus to Captain Kirk.

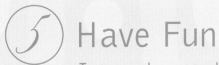

5 Have Fun

Two words a swell should never utter: "I'm bored."

Kids'll break into an impromptu happy dance at the sight of a bowl of M&M's. They bring the funk with them and don't care if they look queer. Worrying about acting cool all the time turns people into stiffs. A swell isn't afraid to take the mic, dive out of a plane, play bad golf— whatever it takes to rev things up. The squarer the scene, the bigger the challenge: how to get the disco ball rolling?

HAMMING IT UP

Performance anxiety. Guys may get it in the bedroom, but in front of a bunch of people, it's chicks who start pouring flopsweat. Making a toast. Telling a joke. All eyes are on you and suddenly it's like someone pushed your personality mute button. But with a few simple tricks of the trade, you'll have the troops laughing, crying, gasping in awe. Squeeze everything you can out of that limelight—before they hook you offstage.

Everyone's a Comedian

For some reason, girls can remember the socks they wore to their first communion but not a joke they heard five minutes ago. When everyone else is telling them, you don't want to come up empty-handed. You just need *one*, for an ice-breaker or to fill a little dead air on the road with your cranky boss. The next time a joke cracks you up, steal it, and tell it every chance you get, until the punchline is emblazoned on your memory. Spare everyone the apologetic "I'm not sure this is that funny but . . ." intro. And don't be afraid to bomb. Here's a cheat sheet with some delivery cues. No guarantees.

Sick Husband

Couple goes to the doctor. Husband's sick.

(Rule 1: Keep it moving fast: Cut down the "a"s and "the"s.)

Doctor gives him a physical, a whole BATTERY of tests.

(Shout a word sometimes; just to make sure they're paying attention.)

CAT scans, MRIs, a colonoscopy.

(Listing three things helps your rhythm. Words with a "k" sound are funny.)

Week later, doctor calls the wife into the office. Doctor says, "I'm afraid your
husband has an extremely rare blood disease. Incurable."

(Pause for dramatic effect.)

Wife sobs hysterically. "There's no medicine, no treatment?"

"Well," doctor says. "There is one thing that you could do to save him."

Wife looks thrilled. She says, "Anything, Doctor. What is it?"

Doctor says, "If your husband's seratonin can be kept at an extremely high level for one year, he
may live. But you'll have to do everything in your power to make him happy. Cook his favorite
meals. Lavish him with praise. Laugh at his jokes. Don't yell at him when he leaves the
toilet seat up. And most important, you must pleasure him at least three times a day."

(If your audience is leaning forward at this point, it means they can't hear. A little louder!)

"Indulge his every sexual fantasy," doctor tells her. "Anything that in the past you
wouldn't do because it was distasteful or morally repugnant, now you must do for him."

(Throw in a few dirty details here, if you're comfortable "working blue.")

"It's his only chance."

Wife listens gravely then goes home to her husband. Over dinner that night
she tells him, "I talked to the doctor."

Husband is surprised.

"What did he say?" he asks. "What are my chances?"

(A long beat. Look sympathetic, deeply sad.)

"He said you're gonna die."

Diving into the Bomb Shelter

If nobody laughs, either they didn't hear you—*I told you, speak up!*—or they didn't think it was funny. Either way, turning red and apologizing only worsens the cringe-fest. Have a recovery line at the ready to save face, and maybe even tickle out a chuckle. A few ways to go: Repeat the punchline, like they didn't hear it, Letterman-style. Explain the ending like they didn't get it. *You see, she didn't want to have sex three times, so she told him . . . never mind.* Laugh really hard yourself—sometimes it's contagious. Pretend to commit seppuku, the Japanese sword to the gut. Wave and tell them, *Thank you very much, I'll be here all week.*

Is There a Magician in the House?

Remember how endlessly fascinated you were by Uncle Larry, the old guy who could pull coins out of your ears? Now it's your turn. Don't let corny traditions die. Any self-respecting aunt, godmother, or baby-sitter should have a couple of tricks up her sleeveless dress to impress the junior members of the party. They work on taller people, too.

Hanky-panky trick

Hold up a freshly ironed handkerchief, then, pinching the center, lift it. When you let go, the hanky remains miraculously upright in your hand. How?

Cinch. Drape the cloth over your closed left fist, in which you have hidden a tiny tape measure. As you wave your other hand over the hanky, to show there are no strings above or below, turn your closed hand and open it. Then pinch the hankie, and draw the tape up, too. Like a pup tent! Turn this into an R-rated trick by talking suggestively to the handkerchief, like that's what's keeping it up.

Five card stupid

Show five cards to your victim. Ask her to concentrate on one card. Pocket the cards. Ask her to write her card on a piece of paper, fold it, and put it on the table. One by one, pull four cards from your pocket and lay them facedown beside the paper. Then say, "Your card remains in my pocket." Unfold the paper. It says "nine of clubs." She turns up the cards on the table—not there. You reach into your pocket and produce the exact card! How?

When your mark is writing down her card, fan the cards (toward you) and arrange them in consecutive order (five, six, seven, eight, nine) and pocket them (beneath four spare cards from the same deck that you already have in there.) After she places the folded paper on the table, bring out the spare cards and lay them facedown. Say you've got the selected card in your pocket. Let the mark examine the cards on the table and see the selected card isn't there. As she unfolds the paper and reveals her chosen card, calmly count the cards in your pocket: five, six, seven, eight . . . until you reach the right one. Then whip it out. Voilà!

YOU'RE TOAST

The happy occasion has reached dessert and you feel like somebody ought to say something—and that somebody ought to be you. This is no time to be winging it. Chances are you're lightheaded with drink or emotion and have dreaded public speaking since your third-grade report on grizzly bears. Rather than gushing about how so-and-so is *such an incredible person* and so-and-so is *so lucky*, be prepared. Write your toast sober; this is one time when spontaneity should be rehearsed. After you thank the hosts and introduce yourself, stick to one anecdote that tells it all, meaning there's a point at the end—and it's *not*

about you. Any observation, even a small one, can be expanded into a theme to give your toast some structure. Like running banana references, even if you invent the theme yourself: *They met at the produce section of the supermarket / they discovered they were both bananas for Woody Allen movies / now he's at church in a monkey suit / and they're off on their honeymoon—to where else? the (banana) Republic of Ecuador*. Keep it short. After five minutes, wrap it up. Reversals help tie things up. End a laff-filled toast with a sentimental send-off. Or undercut a sappy one with what sit-com writers call the treacle cutter, the little joke that comes after the big gooey message.

The "Unprepared" Toast

Winston Churchill, who knew a thing or two about making speech-es, used to stand in front of a mir-ror reciting, *I did not intend to speak today*. You can pull the same maneu-ver. Go up to the mic and say you didn't have time to write a speech but you have some notes, then uncrumple a few scribbled pages. An easy speech format is The List. At the fiftieth birthday for your aunt

Cynthia's Evil Twin

Ilene: CR's birthday is around the corner and she doesn't want a fuss—just something easy, "like dinner at a restaurant." But she had one of those last year. So we resolve not to throw Cynthia a party at all this year. Instead, we'll fete her evil twin and call her Synthetica. Out go the invites, with a picture of Cynthia doctored into a mugshot of a tat-tooed terror. "You may not know her but the FBI does," it reads. "She's got a body by Implant, lives on alimony and booze." At the restaurant, we liven up the table with fake scars, novelty-shop party favors (bloody knives, fake teeth), and a singalong tribute to the "twins" written to the theme of *The Patty Duke Show*. Sample lyrics: "Cynthia works from morn 'til night / To make those clothes come out just right / But Synthetica wakes and calls her ex to harass him for her monthly checks." By the end of the night, we manage to turn another "dinneratarestau-rant" into a rebelliously uncool revel, which loosened everybody up so much you could hardly tell the happy, peppy birthday girl from her bad-to-the-bone alter ego.

Jane, the famous Miss Perfect, you say you've compiled a list of all her good qualities and unfurl a long scroll of paper. After naming half a dozen, tell 'em "Enough of that" and announce the list you've made of her bad qualities, pulling out half an index card. Another easy routine is the fake document. The love letter, pre-nup, New Year's resolutions you claim to have somehow stumbled upon. Use poetic license here—the more outrageous the document's revelations, the better the toast.

The Wedding Singer

Another way to work your material with an invisible net is to write a song, or rather rewrite someone else's. Take a nursery rhyme or sitcom theme and recompose it with your own lyrics. Choose a funny song that fits the subject: "Frère Jacques" for your friend Sue who is marrying the tall Frenchman she fell for in Paris. Pick out a few key plot points in the romance, starting with how they met *in Gay Paree / Her heart melted like brie*. The genius of this shtick is it doesn't have to be that funny, just recognizable, and people will laugh. If you have stage jitters, rope an equally unprepared friend into a duet.

TURNING THE BEAT AROUND

Eva Gabor on *Green Acres*, Lucy Ricardo, Jeannie (as in *I Dream of* . . .). They were all hausfraus with a talent for transforming mundane afternoons into zany episodes. Only their hairbrained hijinx came from accidental screwups. Yours can be on purpose. To face a day of drudgery, at home or at work, keep a few extra supplies around, like a padded bra to wear grocery shopping. (Loiter in the melon section and see if anyone notices.) Brighten up Monday at the office with a harmlessly evil prank. Drop a pile of candy wrappers in a coworker's wastebasket. Then try to keep a straight face while he swears he didn't eat all those Butterfingers. Whatever dumb gag sets off the laugh track in your head. With enough practice, your antics might even light up the applause sign.

Keeping Fun Things Fun

Just because you're at an officially festive occasion doesn't mean you can't have fun. Find ways to wake up sleepy celebratory traditions (unless you enjoy staring like a zombie at Aunt Naomi's collection of Hummel figurines).

The semi-surprise party

There's something vaguely hostile about dozens of people convincing a close friend that they've forgotten her B-day, while conspiring to hide behind couches in a dark room to embarrass and shock supposed friend half to death by popping out and shouting "Happy birthday." Without the huge covert op, you can still keep the element of surprise. The Birthday Girl knows the where and when, but she won't know about the mystery guest—Miss Dissin, the only cool English teacher at Schreiber High, *whom* you bussed in for the occasion.

Home-for-the-holidays video

Sure, you enjoy catching up with the relatives. But after the fifteenth time hearing that story about the big new promotion, you're sick of it. And it's your promotion! If only you could just hit instant replay. Ahah! Next time you go home, bring a video of yourself giving a life update into the camera. Mark the tape with times in case you want to cue up the "Sitting Next to Al Pacino on the Plane" story, or replay "What Happened to the Nice Doctor from Last Year?"

Family Xmas spectacular

Stringing popcorn, tree-trimming, singing carols. The expectation is that every Christmas should be as reliable as a Perry Como TV special. But even Perry had to change the color of his cardigan from year to year. You can be faithful to traditions without having the family special feel like a rerun. Try out one new thing—or bring back a forgotten old one. Avoid the same old morning rush hour to the tree, borrow a nineteenth-century American custom of hiding the gifts around the house—like an Easter-egg hunt. Grown-ups play too. That way gifts turn up all day long—even in the fake whipped cream pie filled with Cracker Jack–style prizes that you dish out at dessert.

When the wee ones' dreams of a white Christmas don't come true, they'll get excited anyway because it's time for No-Snow Sledding—box-sliding down the golf course hills while having a Bing-along with the boom box playing "White Christmas." A half-time pastime for the football families: Hold a Bubble Bowling Tournament. Rest a fabric-covered board on two chairs, with chopsticks stuck in as goalposts—then blow. The object is to move a soapy sud through the end zone. Concoct new customs no matter what the holiday. Suit up in Pilgrim hats and Indian headdresses on Thanksgiving, play a few blindfolded rounds of pin the head on the turkey.

Extreme bachelorettes

Brides now get pretty much the equivalent of bachelor parties for chicks: They get equally blotto, equally raunchy with strippers, and are subjected to equal quantities of forced fun, bar-crawling like a band of frenzied sorority rushees, making strange men eat their candy necklaces. But if a bachelorette party is really supposed to be the last wiggy blowout before settling down, why not take it to the next level? Kick it up to notches unknown! You want wild and dangerous? Make it meaningful. Prepare her for the big leap by bailing out of a plane at fifteen thousand feet. Or make her bring her piggy bank to the race track and teach her a few things about betting on a winning stud.

Happier Hours

This hallowed after-work unwinding ritual can feel stale as bad pretzels. Shake up your cocktail hours with a change of scenery. Get off the bar stool and smuggle a few beers to the batting cage, the pinball arcade, or laser tag. Stock a cooler with some Gewürztraminer and tailgate at the miniature golf course. Pass a flask around at the planetarium and ask everyone if they can see Uranus.

Heating Up Dinner

At your end of the table, the conversation is deader than the veal shank. Gotta get a hot plate under these buzz killers without resorting to *Read any good books lately?* Have a few galvanizing questions ready: What present did you never get when you were a kid? The wallet personality test: Come up with analyses, e.g., the one with old receipts and expired video cards is clinging to the past; the superneat, overorganized one has no room in it (or the owner's life) for someone else to come in and take up space. If you give 'em everything you got and still no pulse, you can always scare up some action by making a couple of propositions nobody can refuse. These are friendly bets, stunts, table tricks not played for money—unless you're hard up for dough.

Wine bottle wager

That you can take a drink from an unopened bottle of wine, without removing the cork. The payoff: Turn bottle upside down, fill the indentation of the bottle in question with some liquid, and drink.

Napkin wager

That you can hold a napkin at the two ends and, without letting go, tie it in a knot. The payoff: With your arms folded (one hand tucked under the biceps; the other hand over the biceps) grasp the ends of the napkin: then unfold your arms and presto, a lovely knot!

Ye olde coin wager

Eight coins are placed in the form of a right angle with five coins making one leg and four the other. You propose to put five coins in each leg by moving one coin only. The payoff: pick up the last coin in the leg that has five and place it on top of the corner coin.

Giving Him the Fish Eye

Ilene: Out in Queens at a Greek restaurant with a crowd of maybe twenty. Not really close friends, more like acquaintances. We're elbows deep in Retsina and grape leaves when I realize, no wallet. Not inclined to bum dinner from people I barely know, I stare at the whole roasted fish with the huge white eyeball and wonder how much that's going to run us. Then a light bulb. I turn to the somewhat delicate-looking lawyer on my left.

"Hey, Eddie, how gross is that fish eye, huh?"

"Pretty gross," he observes, agreeably.

"Bet you your dinner tonight, you won't eat it."

"Eat what?"

"The fish eye!" I raise my voice a little, so the whole table hears the challenge. "Eat the eye and I'll buy you dinner. My treat."

He makes a face. "*You* eat it. I'll buy *you* dinner, if *you* eat the fish eye." Tasted good, too!

Where'd the water go? wager

That you can transfer the water in a saucer to a glass without moving the saucer. The payoff: Hold a lighted match under the glass for a few moments; then place the inverted glass in the saucer, and the water will mysteriously be drawn to it!

A final wager

That your pal can't put on his coat alone. The payoff: every time he starts putting on his coat, you do so, too. Hah!

PLAYMATE OF THE YEAR

Some rules aren't meant to be broken. No one wants to play with the spaz who picks the cards off the poker table with her long red fingernails and ends up showing her hand. Miss Do-Over could just have slid the cards across the felt like a pro and held them close to her vest—if she'd only known how. Here, some tips for rookies trying to break into the game.

The 21 Club

Forget trying to beat the house, count cards, or clean up. The first goal for the newcomer to the blackjack table is not to make enemies.

In Vegas, they deal you two cards faceup and you are not allowed to touch them. In Reno, they deal them facedown. Pick them up but with one hand only (or the guys watching through the overhead cameras will think you're working a scam). Even though there are other players at the table, you're only betting against the dealer to see whose cards add up to 21, or closest to it without going over and losing. Face cards count as 10. An ace is either a one or eleven—it's up to you. To "hit" (take another card), you either point with your index finger or, if you're holding the cards, scrape them toward you. To "stick" (no more cards), wave your hand once over the cards or slide them under your chips.

Take as many cards as you like, but keep in mind, the rest of the table is watching! Novice moves annoy the hardcore players because they are superstitious and think that taking an extra card you shouldn't or not taking one you should have taken messes up the "fate of the deck"—and their hands. Follow these rules to avoid dirty looks.

- If the dealer is showing a 6 or less and you have 13 or more, stand: Because the dealer must hit on anything up to 16, the odds are that he will go over 21. Really good players have nerves of steel, and hit on 16 when the dealer is showing a 7 or higher—because they always assume the dealer's down card is worth 10, the most common card value in the deck.

- Splitting is complicated, but if you don't split eights or aces, people will look at you funny (16 is a crummy hand; an 8 is more promising). Separate them side by side and place another bet in front of the second hand.

- Always double down (or double your bet) when you have an 11. Put the chip *beside* the original bet.

  The dangerous place to sit is in the last seat on the dealer's right. It's the hot seat, because it's the last spot before he draws his own cards. If you make a false move—say draw a 10 and bust—and that 10 would have busted the dealer—the table will want to kill you, even though it's not your fault.

Winning Friends

As intimidating as it can seem, the blackjack table can also be a place to make friends. When 008, James Bond's younger; cuter brother, takes a seat beside you, make the game more exciting by betting on him. Place a chip neatly inside his box, then if he wins his line, so do you. Another thing: Wear a watch, or you'll be bugging other players for the time, since casinos never have clocks or windows. When it's time to cut your winnings, tip the dealer a few chips and cash in the rest!

Golf Berlitz

Most golfers suck, unless they're pros, even the ones who play all the time. Really, 85 percent of them can't break a hundred. The game is maddening, but that's its allure. Hit one good shot and you'll spend the rest of your life trying to do it again. So even if you consider yourself a sub-par or non-golfer, take the next invitation to tag along. You can still be a fun fourth by keeping in mind three things: (1) don't slow the game down; (2) don't mess up the other players; (3) do throw around the goofy lingo like a pro.

At the tee-off, avoid teeing off the other players. Talking when someone's about to swing at the ball is a no-no, and never stand behind another player. If your ball curves left, you've hit a "hook." If it veers right, it's a "slice" or "banana." A ball that barely gets off the tee is a "worm burner." Take a "mulligan," a do-over. (You usually get one in a friendly game.) If a player scoots one along the fairway that barely gets higher than the grass, light mockery is appropriate: "Ladies way up!" or "Does your husband play golf?" (Most golf humor is misogynistic—work with it.) On the fairway, always replace your divots: Put back any hunks of sod you hack up. If you hit a sand trap, announce, "Pass the beach towel!" On the way out of the trap, rake away your footprints. When you close in on the green, you'll need your pitching wedge to hit out of the tall grass and your putter. When you go a-putting, leave the wedge on the "pin" (the flag) that's been pulled out of the cup and left on the apron (the grass around the green). That's the surest way not to forget your wedge after finishing the hole—other players get peeved when they have to drive back to the hole to retrieve it. On the green, don't drop your bag or cross the "lines" between the player's ball, and the cup. (Your footprints will screw up their putt.) If your ball is in the way of someone else's, "mark" it by replacing it with a coin until it's your turn.

Try not to take the game *too* seriously. If the putt's a little shy, concede the final stroke as a "gimme" (anything within a foot of the cup). If you're still on the fairway after "laying" five shots, grab the ball and say, "Picking up." If you're playing slowly and can feel a foursome behind you breathing down your neck, when you step off the green wave at them to "play through." (They cut ahead while you wash your ball, have a soda, and trade bad golf jokes.)

Minnesota Slim

Vamps splaying themselves across a pool table look hot in movies, but real-life sharks will be more impressed by good form: balanced stance, legs comfortably apart, head bent over the cue, gripped not too tightly (with thumb, index, and middle fingers) and never on the "butt plate," the end of the stick. Your arm is perpendicular to the floor, so it can swing like a pendulum. The other hand forms a "bridge" to guide the cue stick. A closed bridge is more secure, the heel of the hand and last three fingers planted on the table, thumb and index finger circling the stick—a full eight inches from the white cue ball.

Now spank that ball, gentle but firm! Where you hit it is going to affect how the ball spins and where on the table it stops spinning. For solid contact, the center is the ideal place to hit. Above center, and it'll spin forward or "follow" and keep rolling after it hits the contact ball, the stripe or solid. Below center, it'll "draw" and stop dead on contact. "English" means hitting the left or right side of the cue ball for sidespin. "Bank" shots are when you ricochet the cue ball off the cushion to make your shot.

What's with the chalking? A cue is like an emery board. After an hour or so of use, it gets smooth and loses its grab. Chalk gives the friction you need to hit without slipping. That way you won't "scratch," whiff the shot by slipping off the cue ball, so that it rolls an ineffectual, embarrassing inch or two. (Unlike golf, pool is a game where you don't want to be a scratch player.)

Darts, Innit?

The best back of the bar time-waster next to pinball and, uh, drinking, started in a pub in Lancashire when a carpenter invented the game in 1896. Don't be intimidated by the weekend dart warriors hogging the board. Write your name on the chalkboard to challenge the winner. When your turn comes around, step up to the toe line, or "oche" (pronounced "ock"), and "bull off." Each player throws and whoever lands closer to the bull's-eye goes first. But familiarity with obscure darting terminology won't get you there.

Darts have four parts: the needle, the body (the brass part with the grip), the shaft, and the flight (the real or fake feathers). Don't clench it like a pencil, but hold it lightly aloft with the thumb, index, and middle fingertips. The elbow is your pivot. Release the dart just before fully extending the arm, then follow through, or the dart will take a nosedive. It's all in the wrist action! The "clock" (board) is about eight feet away and divided into a twenty-piece, numbered pie. The 20 is the "top," the upper section around it is called "upstairs"; the lower part "downstairs." The left half is alleged to be the married man's side (no nickname for the right). Each turn gets three throws to try and hit around the board from numbers 1 to 20. Hitting in the outer ring doubles your score for the shot; the inner ring triples it. A bull's-eye is 50 points, just outside it is 25. When you do score a bull, turn to your mates and say in a surprised Cockney accent, "Darts, innit?"

Craps: The Game That Floats

A coupla dice in your bag and you've got action wherever you go. Craps is a betting game. It is played in casinos, prison, back alleys, or it could "float" to your backyard. The more players, the merrier—because the pot gets bigger with each sucker, uh, player in the game.

Playing for money on unlicensed premises is, of course, strictly illegal. But you can still set a backstop for some dice to bounce against. A cereal box, even (there's no law against cereal boxes). And—hey!—you've got yourself a "bone-yard," as it's known from the days when dice were made from bones or ivory. First, the shooter calls her bet. "I'll shoot five," she says. "Who'll fade me?" That means she's betting five, uh, jelly beans that she'll make her roll, and is inviting other people to bet that she won't. The other players chime in, "I'll take it," and put in five jelly beans each (more or less), whereupon the shooter rolls the dice, the goal being to not "crap out."

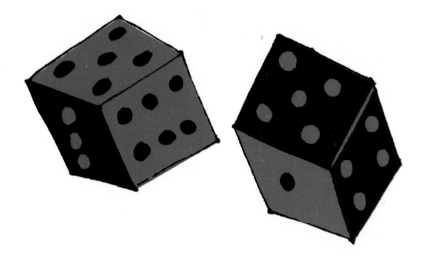

If she rolls 7 or 11, that's a "natural," an automatic win. If she rolls a 2 (snake eyes), 3, or 12 (box cars), she craps out, loses the pot, and can either pass the dice or place a new bet and try again. If she rolls any number other than the aforementioned winners and losers, that's her "point." Then it's a race to roll that number again *before* rolling a 7 in order to "make her point" and win! She can then either "let it ride," i.e., bet her winnings on another round, or pass the dice. A shooter only loses the dice when she doesn't make her point, or stops betting. At the outset, the odds are in your favor. A 7 is the most common combination. But if you don't roll 7 the first time, and have to "make it the hard way," the odds are against you. That's when you have to start blowing on the dice, or singing to them, kissing them, nursing them, and cursing them if they misbehave. Luck be a lady, tonight!

Hooking a Worm

If you've gone fishin', for gosh sakes, hook your own dang worm. Reach into that can of hookass and grab yourself a wriggler. A hooked worm should still look real alive to a hungry fish. So, don't go making yourself a worm kebab, thread the li'l guy back and forth a bunch of times so it's on the hook securely but keeps its curvy shape. And leave some wiggle on the bottom—but not so much that the fish can steal an hors d'oeuvre without so much as kissing the hook.

Here's something else: Wear long flashy earrings. It's a fine substitute when someone loses a lure. Offer him "Lefty's Revenge." All lures have funny names.

Campfire Joe

When the rest of the mountaineers are pitching tents and fetching kindling, offer to make a pot of coffee. The best way to boil coffee is to build a little three-sided stove from stones and mud, saving the flattest rocks for the top layer. Make the walls about six inches high with enough space in the center for a baby fire. When it's cooking, rest the pot on the top of the stones. This prevents the smoky taste coffee gets if it's cooked right on the fire. Oh, and on the hiking trail don't pee anywhere closer than sixty feet from the trail—it attracts bears.

HIT PAUSE

It's all swell and good to repress your inhibitions and maximize your fun, but the twenty-four-hour cruise director who's always "on" is exhausting to be or be around. Equally good company is the chum who can do nothing well, linger over dinner, sit on the porch with a lemonade watching the flies, ride the lulls in a conversation without rushing to fill dead air. So call your boyfriend and make a date to take a long nap, or just hit the couch right now. Zzzzzz.

6 Style

Not just another pretty dress

abulousness, darling! It's all about peplums and shoulder pads.

Chartreuse is the new black this season. A bateau neck with a three-quarter sleeve on a five-eighths coat with a full-circle skirt? Forbidden! Leopard is my passion this spring. Fashion tortures us, yet it makes us weep. . . .

YIKES! Scary fashion divas dictating musts and nevers are enough to make you want to pull a muumuu over your head and whimper, *Why bother?*

Because you feel like a million bucks when you look like it. The dictionary defines the original swell as a "person of distinction or ability, first-class person, member of good society, person of dashing or fashionable appearance." They're the people Cole Porter wrote songs about and Fred Astaire dressed and danced in the image of. Subsequent swells kept the tradition alive by paying fastidious attention to the cut of a jacket, a cuff link's polish. Porter wore eighteen-karat-gold collar stays. Cary Grant would measure the lapels of his suits with a ruler and send them back to the tailor if they were even an eighth of an inch off. "It takes five hundred small details to make one favorable impression," he said. Frank Sinatra's advice? Avoid sitting down and you won't wrinkle your pants. This wasn't just to impress dames. They did it for themselves, taking deep pleasure in superficial wardrobe details. Ladies, take note.

Being well turned out means luxuriating in your clothes, dressing up any room you walk into. Some say you have to be born with style. *Pshaw.* Think of your closet the way a designer puts together a show: storming through outrageous ideas, narrowing down the looks to the best colors and silhouettes, and not being afraid of a few dogs.

PUTTING ON YOUR SHOW: The Four Phases

Not to sound superficial, but you can't get away from the fact that the way you look says a lot about who you are. Everybody's got different sides and different moods, but style is something else. It's a mix of who you were, who you are, and who you want to be.

Phase 1: Identity

Who am I? As existential dilemmas go, fashion's an easy one. Pull up a couch, close your eyes, and ask yourself some questions: What color cheers me up? What pants am I most comfortable in? What fabric always feels great? Unrepress the glamorous self-image buried in your unconscious.

Find your common denominator, then multiply

You love shift dresses, so have weekend shift dresses, daytime shift dresses, and evening shift dresses. Some may be longer, some more bare, but they're all still basically your dress. If you're addicted to slim pants, corner the market. In spring they're showing a little more leg, and in fun fabrics. In fall they're longer and more subdued. Tailor your clothing to your body, not the other way around. If you have a power bootay, and the confidence to match, make a clingy skirt your deadliest weapon.

Let the moods swing

Everyone occasionally wakes up thinking, *Wanna change my hair, my clothes, my face* (as The Boss sang). But you don't want to look like Miss Patchouli one day and

Jackie O the next. You may want to even out the extreme mood swings with a little fashion Prozac. Wearing a poncho doesn't necessitate Birkenstocks, love beads, and a fanny pack filled with granola. Turn the hippy vibe haute with your most sophisticated tube dress. Should you rise from a nap feeling like the heroine of a Jane Austen novel and reach for your muslin petticoat, halt before adding thine antique blouse and pearls. Get ahold of yourself—and something from this century. A comfy little tee will do just fine.

Glamouflage

If you're Miss Casual most of the time, there's no reason to turn into Princess Grace every time the invitation says black tie. You're going to a wedding, not joining the witness protection program. Just doll up the same thing you always wear. If it's T-shirts, make it a silk one. Out of pants and you panic, pull on tuxedo trousers with high shoes. If you feel more at ease when gussied up, don't peer-pressure yourself into dressing down. Sell your fashion soul and you'll end up like one of those people who wear suntan panty hose and shorts at a clambake. You'll be cooler wearing the sexy dress with no makeup and bare feet.

Phase 2: Use Your Own Ideas

Just because puce is in, doesn't mean it's in your wardrobe. Fads and trends come and go. If you copy them head to toe from the magazines you'll just look like every other kid on the block.

You find this old picture of yourself at camp when you were ten, wearing a pair of madras shorts, and you're amazed: *Wow, I looked cool.*
Revive your own groovy childhood self and make your spring look "all about" madras. Hit vintage shops, Brooks Brothers, or maybe go back to your home-

town where Chucks Men's Wear still carries all the same stuff. Settle on a boy's madras jacket to throw on over your little bare dresses all summer long.

Teacups on Your Head

Cynthia: *Inspiration can come from anywhere. A book you just read on gypsies. The sparkly stuff in the asphalt outside your house. The cool iridescent color of tropical fish. Ideas are everywhere. The question is, which one takes the cake? Walking past a bakery, I noticed the birthday cakes in the window with those cute blue and pink roses. Hmmm . . . desserts. Which reminded me that I owed a lot of people dinner, maybe because I was reading Emily Post's etiquette book at the time. Then I got the "Aha!" moment. A runway like a banquet table! And models wearing the dessert— sweet little cocktail confections in frosting colors. White "napkin" halter tops, fork-and-knife hair combs. . . . When I got to the doggy bag evening purses made out of aluminum foil, I knew I'd gone too far. Whether it's on the runway or just your look of the day, try to keep something of the original inspiration, without spinning out of control. I ended up doing trousers, sweaters, parkas in crisp tablecloth white—winter white—and allowed myself one indulgence: a jaunty teacup hat.*

You notice the three Jelly Beans sitting in the bottom of your purse and suddenly you think, Mmm, they look good enough to wear.

So, now as you set out to add a few basics to your spring wardrobe, instead of buying them in the usual easy-to-match navy, tan, and white, make Jelly Belly lemon, lime, and orange the season staples. Rediscover the rainbow Izod shirts and Ballantine sweaters. Mix them together, cut the brightness with white.

You take a trip to the islands in the winter where the native women wear really pretty, lacy cotton dresses.

Problem is they just graze the knee, and long is the new length this spring. So don't buy one—buy two and head to the tailor! (Essential as a good lawyer.) Have one cut down, add an extra eighteen inches to the other—poolside panache.

Phase 3: Risks

When you're a kid your ideas about what matches and what is proper are krazy! Defiantly mixing plaids, trying to turn a necklace into a headband, bleaching holes in jeans because it looks cool. *Why grow up?*

Rejuvenate your approach

Rethink the things you look at every day, whether they belong in your wardrobe or not. Don't have the right belt for those high-water trou? Grab the clothesline out of the shower and wrap it through your belt loops a couple of times. Get dressed wrong. Audrey Hepburn used to wear her cardigans backward, and just for kicks would turn a man's Oxford into a wrap-around shirt, unbuttoned and cinched in the back. So, get added mileage from a tired slip dress by wearing it under a turtleneck. *Eureka!* The waistless skirt you never knew you needed for a visit to an all-you-can-eat buffet. Can't sort out the Monday morning blues? Clash freely—cornflower, cobalt, navy, periwinkle. Break the rules, but not all at once. (You want to look lawless not clueless.)

Take a chance on something safe

When Talking Heads came on the scene at the height of the punk movement, they outdid the green Mohawk and safety-pin club kids by wearing chinos and button-downs on stage. When everyone's trying to one-up each other with novelties and gimmicks, the most outlandish thing you can wear is something traditional. Be radical by dusting off your old Bass Weejuns, Cousin Helen's cowboy boots, or Grandma's garnet brooch (pin it to the tiny strap of a bare evening dress).

Phase 4: Edit!

Sometimes the best thing for your look is the piece you leave behind. Love it but leave it. Be ruthless. Make war on your sartorial excesses and peace of mind will follow.

Closet triage

Clutter is the enemy. You can't have a vision if you can't see your forest-green slacks through the shoe trees. At the end of each season, take stock. Set expiration dates. If at first you wore it weekly, then bimonthly, now you trot it out once a season—it's sad but over. The cashmere wrap skirt you adore, with *only one* moth hole. Say thanks for the memories! Even in war, however, there are acts of sympathy. The sequin snakeskin blazer so wiggy you gotta keep it for your grandchildren. . . . Archive it along with the other museum-quality pieces. Stick it somewhere the sun don't shine (a garment bag) and wait 'til it's vintage. Just so long as it doesn't interfere with the stuff you are going to wear in this millennium.

Don't primp. Prune.

Before you walk out the door, *take one thing off*. When you look in the mirror, pick your point of focus. If it's the silver shoes, let them shine. Meaning no competition from rhinestone hair baubles or a couple of cocktail rings. The exception to this rule is when you're trying to make the room temperature rise. Then put something back on. If you're trying to look hot, leave something to the imagination. Tush, cleavage, *and* navel gazing? Too much. Limit yourself to one exposure per outfit.

BUYING TIME

Contrary to Smokey Robinson's mother's anthem, it's not always better to shop around. You love the thrill of the acquisition, the rush of the cash flow. But if it's a sunny afternoon, who wants to be aimlessly looking at belts and Velcro?

- Have a purpose

  Avoid buying crap you don't need. Don't wait for a sale, because any thing you liked will be gone by then. Likewise, don't spend weeks hunting for something slightly better or cheaper. If you know you love it, get it now. Buy two. Men always do.

- Come armed

  When you walk into a boutique, not just with plastic but the newspaper ad or magazine shot of the item you're coveting. You can even call ahead. If they have it, ask them to put it aside. Buying shoes to go with a dress? Bring the dress. Try on the whole look in the store.

- Dress to shop

  You'll feel more stylin' and get better service.

- Take their card

  It doesn't hurt to buddy up with the salespeople at your regular haunts: Ask their names; ask if they're selling what they have on. Next time you walk in—instead of hearing those tragic words "sold out," wouldn't it be nice to hear, "Look what I saved for you."

Prisoner of Seventh Avenue

Ilene: *Friendship has its privileges. Many a time Cynthia has prepped me for the big event, big interview, big date. I'll arrive at her showroom on Seventh Avenue, look around thinking there's nothing that seems right for the occasion, then she blitzkriegs through the sample racks and pulls together the just-right outfit I never would have seen. Of course, the downside of her watchful eye is that I can't get away with any of my miscreant fashion behavior. Just try showing up at Rowley HQ in a pair of last season's glassphalt gray pants, now baggy in the butt. Her eyes narrow: "Will you get rid of those!" But I've learned a thing or two from my fashion parole officer.*

Lose the jewelry

I used to get dressed, comb my hair, then put on my jewelry—all of it. Graduation ring, the s-chain from Mom, the zirconium studs Aunt Sheila gave me. When Cynthia would come pick me up, I'd ask, "How do I look?"

"Great," she'd say, "but maybe leave out the necklace, and how would it look without the bangle bracelets?" For years, she wouldn't let me wear jewelry at all. (Meanwhile, in her last show there were beaded hoops that reached down to the shoulder and that was OK.) But she has a point: Wearing your whole jewelry box can make you look like a Christmas tree.

Wear sexy shoes

Countless times I would try on a dress and hear Cynthia say, "Cuuuute—with a pair of sexy, sexy shoes." Not sure what that meant, I'd go out and buy yet another pair with chubby heels and thick soles. Ugly shoes were my compulsion. Finally, Cynthia dragged me by my ear to Barney's and explained the facts of shoes: sexy ones have slender heels, pointy toes, and are "strappy, strappy." Sure, there's a place for chunky platforms, and the Japanese clogs she's been wearing lately are sexy in an offbeat way. But with sex and shoes sometimes you have to be direct, ask any fetishist.

Mess things up, roll things up:

Cynthia always has a way of looking kind of neat yet casual at the same time. This, I've decided, is because she rolls things up—tube socks, the bottom of a T-shirt. And to keep from looking too prissy, she'll mess something up—push up the sleeves of a sweater with an evening dress. Or roll down the elastic smocking of a big red sun dress, and wear it like a skirt with a bikini top, only to reappear later with it rolled back into a dress.

Break up the set

Trying to look put together, the temptation is to try to wear things that go together. In the showroom, when Cynthia and I are getting ready to go out, she'll hold up, say, a fleur-de-lys halter dress and say "How 'bout this?" Instinctively, I grab for the matching jacket nearby, but she's not interested: "Too trying too hard." Just because it goes, doesn't mean it goes. "Because then it's an outfit, it's an ensemble," she explains, as if those were dirty words. So sometimes if it goes . . . it's gotta go.

HAVE A SIGNATURE

Diana Vreeland had red, from the blush on her cheeks to the paint in her apartment. Carrie Donovan has the big-frame eyeglasses. Every fashion diva has one. It doesn't matter if it's your hairstyle, your cinnamon scent, or your penchant for wearing nothing that matches, but have one thing you're remembered for. Maybe you only carry vintage bags. Maybe you're known for wearing bare-backed dresses. But adopt at least one item that outlives trends, something that becomes you, and make it your John Hancock.

BUY A NEW T-SHIRT

Sure, you could drag out last year's model and douse it with bleach. But styles change in subtle ways, and so does your eye. Update your classics. Collars that looked great two seasons ago seem slightly off today. Suddenly your trusty black pants don't have enough flare or flair. That's fashion's insidious effect on our psyches. You are hereby absolved of any guilt for retiring that "perfectly fine" black miniskirt and replacing it with a slightly slimmer edition, or trading up your yellowing white shirt for a crispy new one with wider collar and longer cuffs. Who wants to start a season wearing a bunch of her own hand-me-downs?

HAVE AN ACE IN THE HOLE

Mix and match all you like, but every season have one outfit that you know works head to toe. This is your jump-into suit, the quick saver for a last-minute invite, the speed change when you get home with twenty-five seconds to spare before running out again. No swell sits home because she has "nothing to wear."

Wrap It Up

You fret over the details of an elegant evening getup, then put on a ten-year-old wool coat. The shame! For all those entrances and exits, velvet ropes and last glances, a shlubby black coat is not the image you want to present. This is the first thing people see when you walk in the door. And if you're party-hopping it might be all they see. So don't skimp on outerwear. Have options. Instead of adding to your museum of scarves, invest in wraps, which never go out of vogue. In cashmere, pashmina, or shatoosh (shhh! only available on the blackmarket), wraps are an excellent evening-coat alternative. But even if you love it, check it at the door. Otherwise, it ends up on the floor or draped over your arm the whole night, like you're some kind of human towel rack.

⑦ Be Lucky

When it comes to luck, a swell leaves nothing to chance

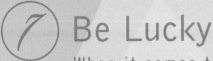

WORK THE MOJO

Life's a smorgasbord for bellyachers, an endless buffet of tightwad bosses, lost earrings, exploding pens. There's always something to be depressed about. But that's so . . . depressing. Snap out of it! Being swell isn't just about smooth moves and booze, it's about having the right spirit. Chin up, as they used to say. We call it pathological optimism. Either way sounds corny. But it's the soul of swell: knowing how to make the bad times good and the good times unforgettable.

How often do tarot cards and psychic networks deliver anyway? Develop talent for reading your fortune in the here-and-now! When Fate smiles on you, it would be rude not to smile back. So spin-doctor the bad news so it sounds good even if it requires creative interpretation. Lose your wallet? Chance for a better driver's license photo. Or you're booked as a guest on a late-night TV show then bumped. . . .

"Cynthanea Crowley"

Cynthia: *An invitation came to go on the David Letterman show. "Dynomite!" It seemed too cool to be true. And it looked like maybe it was. They'd never had a designer on the show before. The producers wanted to know what I could talk about. Did I have any good material? (And they didn't mean a few yards of crêpe de chine.) So I laid everything on them—embarrassing Girl Scout moments, even my top-secret inventions (like the revolutionary double-sided "toothbrush for lovers."*

I was in! Awaiting my turn in the greenroom, I was aflutter with nerves, or maybe just the subzero A/C. I listened to the Top 10 List, then Paul Shaffer, then the other guests. David Brenner was still joking about his son's bar mitzvah when Dave interrupted to say good night, apologizing that there was no time left for "Cynthanea Crowley." I'd been bumped.

Everyone assumed I'd feel like a humiliated loser. But I thought, What a break! Like I'd prepared for a test I didn't have to take. "Next time I won't be so nervous," I said.

Couple of months later, I got my three minutes with Dave. And I was ready, even though Dave never asked about any of my inventions. He wanted to talk fashion after all, like why designers put models in ridiculous things no one would ever wear, with "titanium fins sticking out of their backs." He was suddenly Elsa Klensch. I winged it. I have no idea what I ended up saying, but at least I knew enough to wear long sleeves—and a bra—so people wouldn't see my goose bumps.

MAGICALLY DELICIOUS

Hearts, moons, Grandpa's police badge

It never hurts to blow on the dice. Even Nobel-Prize winning physicists have been known to have a rabbit's foot hanging over the door of the lab. But mix the traditional with your own magic formulas: If a white cat crosses your path—it's good luck. Why shouldn't it be a good sign if a black cat is supposed to be bad? Superstitions are open to interpretation. Even triskaidekaphobia, fear of the number 13. Most people think the indivisible figure that never appears in elevators is the jinxiest number going. But it was pretty lucky for those colonies in 1776. (Then again, it wasn't so good for the British.)

Charm School Lessons

Hung like a horseshoe

Girls love horses. What better get-lucky symbol to mount over the bed? But hang it open side up or the luck runs out—and so might the stud you corraled from the herd.

Four-leaf clover

The only green thing Eve took with her from Eden, one legend has it. Good luck finding the mother of lucky charms. Still, taking a memento from your own paradise is not a bad idea: a piece of coral from the Caribbean, a bread pudding crock nicked from that seaside bistro in Lisbon, or a bottle cap picked up at a party—nail it to the wall next time you throw one.

Penny-wise

Pick it up only if it's heads-up. Two heads are better than one, so glue a couple of coppers together and keep them in your purse. Never give a wallet as a gift without including a penny or other coin. If you give a knife, a coin has to be exchanged, too, or your relationship with the recipient is in danger of being severed. If you're planning to jilt the guy after the holidays, give him a pocket knife for Christmas and keep the change.

Skeleton by the bed

They say the way to scare away a ghost is to look him in the eye and boldly ask, *What do you want?* Instead of trying to steer clear of the things that scare you most, a swell move is to make 'em familiar. Wounded by a childhood bus accident, the fiesta-loving artist Frida Kahlo endured countless grave operations throughout her life. She kept a skeleton by the side of her bed, and every morning when she woke, she shook its hands and said, *"Hola, 'mana"* (Hiya, sister).

Gems

They have value beyond their retail worth. Amethyst prevents drunkenness, rubies bring peace of mind, sapphires help you sleep, emeralds conjure excellent memory.

Acorn

A totem of strength from the mighty oak, which is why they're sometimes on the pullstring of a window shade: to protect the house from storms.

Grandpa's police badge

Collect things from people with good vibes. Aunt Flora's cigarette case, a baseball card of your Yankee idol, a wallet photo of Amy, the pet collie who chaperoned you to school when you were a pup.

Touching Up Your Photographic Memory

Famously lucky people have selective memories. This is easier to do if you make the good scenes really memorable. When things are going right, stop the action, take a mental snapshot. Work on building your lucky legend with the stories you tell. "I guess I must have had someone watching over me from the day I was born, because I seem to have made the right move every time," said Frank Sinatra. He was talking about his decision to leave the Tommy Dorsey Band and strike out on his own—the move that turned him into a huge pop star. But where was the guardian angel for his first tour, with The Hoboken Four, three truck drivers, two of whom supposedly *used* Sinatra as a punching bag, or when he was plugging local radio stations, singing for free and never earning more than bus fare home? Irrelevant. To Frank, the move that made him the biggest star of his day wiped out all that other jazz. In the mental home movie of your life, you're the director, it's all in the editing. The same story could be spliced together like a clip reel from the six o'clock news, one disaster after another; or you could put a little Spielberg in your biopic and sell lots of popcorn.

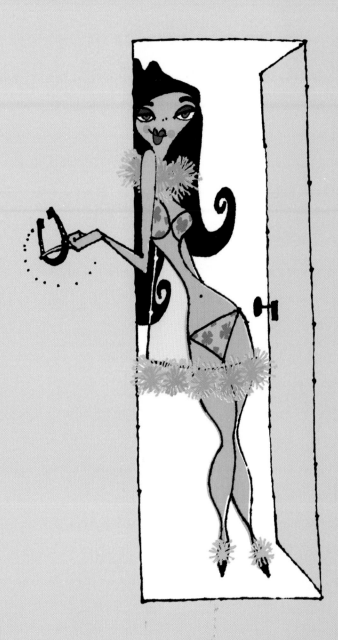

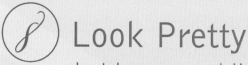

8 Look Pretty

Just because a girl's got a big caboose
doesn't mean she can't be a looker

A great beauty cannot be measured by the sum of her anatomically correct parts. She's got to have *that certain something*. What that certain something is can be tricky to pin down. But as near as we can figure, polish, posture, and personality are a good place to start. It's all in there somewhere. Just tease it out.

POLISH

Scratch a bombshell, find a rocket scientist. Or at least a chemistry whiz, capable of performing amazing feats of haironautical engineering requiring dizzying computations of root volumizer divided by silicon gel and unknown variables like barometric frizz factors—all without a calculator. A swell girl doesn't let this kind of genius go to waste!

All brilliant scientists rejected the conventional wisdom of their time: Newton, Einstein, Estée Lauder. Likewise, the Swell Beauty Theoretician realizes that the dictum that women should engage in a lifelong quest to maximize "assets" and minimize their "flaws" is based on faulty logic. How can there be one way to calculate the perfect eyebrow if Greta Garbo got away with pencil drawings and Brooke Shields was worshipped for her shrubbery? If you've been hiding under bangs your whole life trying to distract attention from a

bumpy nose, part your hair down the middle, showing off the honker to full effect. Paint on a Parisian pout and decide you've got a Left Bank look for now. Flaws can be considered *assets*. It's all a matter of perspective.

Whatever the "problem," learn to experiment. Your chemistry set may blow up a couple of times, but that's the price of entering the Vanity Science Fair. Here are a few blue-ribbon prizewinners.

Gravity-defying boobs

Going strapless or backless? Create the illusion of buoyancy with remarkably simple tape technology: one or two strips of electrical or masking adhesive that go from one armpit to the other, pressed beneath the breasts in the same line as underwire would go, thus pushing them up and together. Caution: De-stickify tape on fabric before applying to skin, so as not to remove boob when removing tape.

Invisible makeup

At the gym, on a camping trip, there are times when wearing makeup makes a girl look like she's got something to hide. No one will detect these invisible tricks: a touch of eyelash glue in the brows and brush with a toothbrush to hold them in the finished shape; line lips and fill in with neutral pencil then coat with lip balm; a few dabs of blush before moisturizer.

Cryogenics

An EZ answer to awaken a dead complexion. Rub an ice cube over your face before makeup and watch skin tighten and circulation increase in seconds. Marilu Henner and Joan Crawford's trick.

This experiment posits that the subject wears one pair of sunglasses (the constant) and only the lipstick is variable (x factor). The equation can yield multiple look solutions.

X-1: Bee stung, a.k.a. the Rosebud. The original silent screen pucker, created by Max Factor, when pre-lipstick pommade couldn't touch the corners of the mouth or it would run into the greasepaint. Dip thumb into pot of gloss or rouge and press two thumbprints on upper lip, then turn thumb upside down and press into lower lip. With a brush, spread it out a little.

X-2: Marilyn. A perfectly defined silhouette in reddish pink or gold; for extra oomph, she lavishly shined with Vaseline to create a round, voluptuous effect.

X-3: Mod Mouth. Pale gloss, from Julie Christie's frosty white to Jackie O's dewy tawny shade.

X-4: Disco Slut. Two words: fuchsia shock.

X-5: Almost Collagen. Darker/brighter shades make lips more prominent, so does applying liner slightly outside lips' contours. A dab of white in the center of the lower lip makes the mouth look fuller.

X-6: Lasagne Lips. Rich and delicious. Apply lipstick, pat gently with tissue, then apply translucent powder, add another layer of lipstick, powder, lipstick. Stays on from the pasta through the dolci.

Optical illusions

- White away!: Visine, and white eye pencil to line lower inner lid. Pale blue can work too. Makes the whites look brighter.
- The "Banane": French bombshell Brigitte Bardot had one easy-to-copy curve—the liquid liner along the top lid. Pull lid to temple, paint, let dry, release.
- Natural false eyelashes: Cut strip of lashes into tiny sections, pick each up with tweezers, brush them and natural lashes with mascara before applying. Wait a moment to allow glue to get sticky, apply shortest lashes where your own are shortest, longest at the center. For a dollish expression add longest lashes to the corner of the lower lid á la Twiggy. Apply more mascara once they're on. Then curl.
- Faking false lashes: Predust lashes with baby powder, then a couple of coats of mascara.
- Decorative lashes: Apply waxy substance to end of each separate eyelash in the form of a bead. Coco Chanel's models imported this trick from Russia. Man Ray made beaded lashes that looked like tears in his film *Kiki's Double*.

Tantoos

Based on principles of photosynthesis, this semipermanent tattoo uses the skin's natural pigmentation. Cut a piece of masking tape into a heart, a leaf, your boyfriend's initials, a $ sign, or other decorative shape and stick on thigh, tush, or tummy, then tan (or apply self-tanner) and lift off. Eureka! A negative "tantoo."

Runners get shinsplints. The marathon party girl has her own affliction: puffy peepers, or what Holly Golightly called "the mean reds." If you've got all day, you can soothe your lids with chamomile tea bags, cool mint leaves, and cold milk eye baths. But what if you're already tardy for Sunday brunch? Shrug your shoulders. *C'est la vie*. So you'll look sexy in a Simone Signoret kind of way. One of the sexiest French chicks ever, she always looked like she'd been through the wringer. Make the world-weary look work. Spritz hair with styling lotion, flip head over, blast with blow-dryer, tousle so it's good and undone. Throw on a big sweater, letting your lingerie peek through the stretched-out neck. Finger-dab lips with color for the bruised effect, hit the road with perfume on high, voice low and gravelly.

POSTURE

Diana Vreeland said beauty has everything to do with the extension of the neck, arms, back, legs, and a light step. And she was no slouch. So stand up, suck it in, aim your headlights straight ahead, and *think tall*. True self-assuredness can take a lifetime to achieve. Posture you can have in a snap.

Thinking Tall

Women get cold more easily than men. Dressed in sleeveless nothings, we shuffle around, arms crossed, hunched over, looking like li'l ol' arthritic ladies. After checking your coat, whirl arms around to loosen up those shoulders and warm up. Take a few deep breaths. Carry a sweater. Rock-hard abs also make you stand straighter. Sex is an efficient way to strengthen the middle back. Sit-ups and the rowing machine help, too. But yoga really does make you taller.

All that guru-speak about a "golden cord" running through your spine gets into your head until you find yourself realigning automatically. Even when you take a load off there's no excuse for slouching. Save crossed legs for pictures or a bar stool. At a table or desk, sit with one foot in front of the other, on the edge of the chair. Let the rear bones of the pelvis balance your weight, firming your back and preventing unsightly thigh and buttock spread.

Walking

Girls spend zillions on shoes. But there's no point in splurging on an expensive pair of spikes if you pitch forward and race-walk in them like running shoes. Put some hip in your walk and your clothes will look better, too. A sashay in an A-line skirt will make it swing like a ringing bell. A jaunty stride in trousers looks more relaxed if you lean back slightly. A fluid glide in a ball gown and you appear to be floating. Models are told to practice walking around their apartments to music to find their rhythm. The basic supermodel boom-boom: Rotate hips by stepping one foot directly in front of the other—right foot in center, left foot in center, kind of like a sobriety test. Just a hint of catwalk goes a long way.

Posing

These are your memories! Why make them painful? When you're going to be immortalized by Kodak, minimize the double chins. The camera doesn't lie but it *can* fib a bit. To look narrower, swivel shoulders three quarters of the way around. Take a couple of inches off your hips and thighs by standing with one leg in front of the other bent slightly at the knee. Drop your bags, and all the other junk you're carrying, keep the hands free, uncluttered, hide the cocktail behind your back. Now smile. The camera is your friend and your lover. Look deeply into the lens. You've got it now. Groovy. Wild. A little more, baby. A paparazzi trick: If you look a fright or are with someone you don't want to be snapped with, don't get bratty, just close your eyes. They'll never run it in the newspaper, and it won't make the cut in most photo albums either.

PERSONALITY

Having one's not enough. You gotta advertise it. Make yourself a billboard for yourself. Sell, baby, sell, with any gimmick that'll move the product: you!

Smile Hi Club

Europeans can ID Americans at twenty paces, even if they're not wearing Bermuda shorts and a Hawaiian shirt, because they smile so darn much. If a moody pout is a sign of sophistication, a swell is happy to look like a hick with a sense of humor. There's a time for fake smiles, too, like on the phone with a new flame. It's an old salesman's trick. When the face is smiling, the voice sounds more relaxed. In any circumstance, smiling is easier if you use the beauty pageant ploy of applying Vaseline to the teeth. (Not advised if you're planning on kissing the judges.)

Beauty in slo-mo

As a Penthouse Pet once told us, doing things slowly makes them seem sexier. Walking, gesturing, lifting a bite of food to your mouth, languid movements are relaxing. So next time you have to go to the powder room, instead of leaping out of your chair and knocking it backward, downshift. If you find the person across the way is looking at you with a dreamy expression, sit back down and get up again, give him the instant replay.

Sparkle

Some dames light up a room. Marlene Dietrich had her wigs sprinkled with real gold dust. Joan Crawford stuck a diamond on her forehead to distract from the Samsonites under her eyes. They knew that when the inner spark sputters, you still need razzle-dazzle—even if it's only skin deep. Verushka, supermodel of the sixties, would pat her eyes and shoulders with gold leaf—available at any art supply store. Clothes with sheen, Brylcreem to make the hair shine. Glitter Barbie gives skin glow. How do you think she scored Ken?

Something askew

Undoing an extra button to catch someone's eye is so obvious. A more subtle way to get him to do a double take is to do up only one button of your cardigan—the wrong one. There's something sexy about being a little disheveled. Turn a necklace off-center. Be the schoolgirl with one kneesock rolled down. At least it's a conversation starter.

Speak up

The voice is an instrument, learn to play it. People who don't, drift by default into a range populated by ducks, whiners, shrill talkers. Everything sounds better when the words start in the diaphragm, not the sinuses. Frank Sinatra, nicknamed "The Voice," learned control by swimming underwater as long as he could without coming up for air. What made his style so hypnotic, not to mention almost impossible to sing along with, was his phrasing, his inimitable pauses, and surprising inflections. Same rules apply for talking.

The main thing is to get out of your "head" voice and into a deeper chest voice, where richer notes lie waiting to be released. Explore your register. To open up and see what you got in there, try yawning—it relaxes the throat and face muscles, which work together. Or hum, like Enrico Caruso did. If you find a new tone you like—maybe down in the Lauren Bacall end of the register—use it on the hotel manager who lost your reservation or when accepting an offer to cruise the Mediter-ranean with a Greek tycoon.

How you say something will never be quite as important as what you say. So skip swearing. It's the lazy way of sounding colorful. Holly Golightly would have gotten dull fast if she'd been telling stories about all the "assholes" she'd met. She called them "rats" and "super rats." Say more and sound better using your own zinger lingo, and take the edge off taboo subjects like money. Next time the bill arrives and nobody's making the reach, you're ready: "What's this shindig gonna bruise us?" Only a super rat won't understand.

Smell swell

Napoleon wouldn't go into battle without his eau de cologne. Neither should you. Perfume is courage in a bottle. It "heralds a woman's arrival and prolongs her departure," Coco Chanel said. Like poetry, perfume is evocative and capable of stirring strong emotions, one reason you don't want to wear too much on an airplane.

> ### "She Looks So Peaceful"
> **Cynthia:** *The makeup artist has been at it for forty-five minutes, whipping out brushes, powders, pots of gloss, rouge, like some crazed abstract expressionist. It's a big fancy awards ceremony and I'm on in five minutes. I ask for a look in the mirror.* "Not 'til I'm done," *she barks. Ilene checks me out and says, warily,* "You look so . . . brown." *I beg for some* other *color. The artist changes my lips from brown to brownish red, but I still look like a bad oil painting. No time to quibble. Ilene and I beat it to the ladies' room.* "Got any turpentine?" *she asks. We wipe everything off. One minute to award time!* What have we got to work with? *All Ilene's carrying in her lipstick tote is . . . lipstick, Pink 'n' Frosty. Use it! We dab it on my lids, lips, cheeks. Not bad. It even held up under the hot lights. Makeup lesson No. 3541: Just 'cause it's a formal event doesn't mean you have to look like the guest of honor at a wake.*

Perfume, like personality, should change with your mood and the weather. At night in front of a roaring fire when all you're wearing is a bearskin rug, you might prefer to serve yourself up in a full-bodied, red-blooded fragrance. It's cold outside. Bodies don't give off as much energy, so you can go heavier. On a tropical afternoon, when scents carry more bang, keep it light. Something as green and fruity as a poolside salad.

People with a higher percentage of body fat, or with oily or darker skin, retain scent longer, and it smells stronger on them. The thinner, paler, and drier the complexion, the more you may need to refuel, or wear something more high-octane. Parfum is the heaviest, then eau de parfum, eau de toilette, eau de cologne. Calibrate for the occasion. And throw in a curve ball every now and then just to make sure he's paying attention. Dressing in your gray flannel suit, splash a little Old Spice on your pulse points (behind the ears, knees, elbows, wrists, ankles, "anywhere you expect to be kissed," Coco advises).

COMPLIMENTS

People don't give compliments to start an argument. No one who tells you they like your new haircut wants to hear, "Are you kidding? Look at those split ends." Whether it's out of insecurity or some wacko notion of modesty, women often have a bad time handling flattery gracefully. Take compliments at face value. Smile, say thanks, look pleased.

Giving can be as tricky as getting. If your friend in the ladies' room wants to know if her black leather pants are too tight and, indeed, her ass looks like an oil spill, this is no time for the truth. Her only hope is a confidence booster. Spare her the big phony, "You look grreeaat! Rilly!" Create a diversion. Then pick out a small thing that you can honestly say to make her feel good. Say what a cute bag she's carrying. This she'll believe. The smaller the compliment, the more convincing. Even if it's just "Your eyelashes are soooo long."

INSULTS

What about when you run headfirst into a green-eyed cat making clawing remarks. "You look so *tired*." Or, "So, how's the diet?" You don't have to take that! Fight back. Not by counter-scratching, bristling, or running away. Repel the wench without becoming one. Keep asking her to repeat the crack until she feels like a total idiot. The ultimate reversal is the sneak-attack compliment. When she hisses, "I love that dress. I wore it all last year," don't spit back, "Oh, really? Mine's a size 4." Tell her, "You always have the best clothes." If you want to get physical, there's the old Japanese slapstick routine. Jerk your leg up, stopping just short of her groin, then scratch your kneecap innocently, as if you were just making it easier to reach. It works with an "itchy" elbow to the jaw, too.

Whistling Construction Workers

You're a-wigglin' down the block with your heels and head high. Now if you could only get past those hard hats alive. Don't discount compliments just 'cause they come from sweaty guys eating salami for breakfast. They're just saying out loud what the rest of their gender is thinking. If they give you a "Yo, mami. Nice tatas!" shoot back a hearty "Thank you!" and feel free to feel flattered. If it still sounds like you're passing the reptile house at the zoo, flash a fake police badge and keep walking your beat.

Indulge
What to do when dieting on a first date? Cheat!

The best things in life are . . . expensive. They cost, in dollars, calories, time. And they're worth it! What's the point of embalming yourself in bottled water if it means missing out on all the naughty excesses that make your short time on earth worth clinging to in the first place? So jump off the friggin' treadmill. Splurge on room service, even in your own apartment. Bring on the caviar and champagne. Painting the town pink? More truffles! Live a little *now*, pay later. The most appealing girl in the room isn't the sallow-cheeked coat-hanger picking at her salad. She's the bonne vivante who knows the right oysters to order before dinner, how they distill single malt scotch, and how to say yes to dessert.

CHAMPAGNE

What else in life is so glamorous, and yet so silly? It tickles the nose, gives you the giggles (because the CO_2 released from bubbles allows the alcohol to be absorbed by the bloodstream faster). Even Dom Pérignon was acting goofy when he discovered the stuff in the seventeenth century, running to his fellow monks shouting, *"Oh, come queekly, I am dreenking zee stars!"*

Surprisingly, DP is the fanciest but also the flattest. Bubbles aren't everything. By definition, true champagne is made from the li'l champagne grapes grown in the Champagne region of northeast France. Anything else is

sparkling wine. The quality of champagne is measured by sweetness and by bubbles—finer bottles have smaller bubbles and more of them. Generally, the drier
the better—and less headache-inducing. *Brut* is bone dry (less than 2 percent
sugar). Then comes *extra sec* (meaning dry), *sec*, *demi-sec*, and *doux* (very
sweet/dessert wines). The good stuff should be refrigerated only two hours
before serving. Any longer dulls the flavor, which is why a cheap bottle can never
be too cold. Speed-chill in twenty minutes by submerging the bottle in
a bucket filled with ice and water (conducts cold more efficiently than refrigerated air or ice); invert it the last five minutes. When serving, the object is
maximum fizz, minimum spillage, and not killing anyone. There's a pressure of
about seventy pounds behind a cork, so don't shake it up. Slowly turn the bottle,
not the cork, and ease it out with your thumb. Now the glasses. The wide kind
that you see passed around swell affairs in old black-and-white movies were orig-
inally modeled on Marie Antoinette's bosom; pretty shape but they don't keep
the bubbles as well as flutes or tulip glasses. Whichever you use, pour like a stew-
ardess. Start each glass with an inch of wine. After that settles down, go around
and fill all to the brim. If there's leftover bubbly, keep drinking. In an emergency, drop a needle or pin into the bottle and fasten a balloon over the neck
with a rubber band. That should hold 'til you're back from the weekend.

CAVIAR

Besides being an aphrodisiac, and the tastiest cure for a hangover, caviar is a
mighty classy way to egg someone's house. Since the breakup of the Soviet Union,
the traditional source of this delicacy, the world of caviar has descended into
chaos. Iran, China, Kazakhstan, France, and the U.S. are all getting in on the
action. But no matter who's doing the fishing, there are still three basic types.

Beluga

The mother of caviars. These super-expensive, silvery, pearl-size eggs come from a sturgeon that can grow twenty feet long, weigh a ton, and live 150 years. The ones from the Caspian Sea often yield the most succulent, subtly flavored eggs.

Osetra

The sedan-size sturgeon can contain as much as three pounds of golden brown roe. Some chefs prefer these smaller eggs with the nutty rich taste because they're firmer than the pricier beluga.

Sevruga

For mere mortals, tiny near-black, glittering eggs with a deep briny flavor. With all three, the word to look for is "malossol," Russian for "lightly salted," designating the shipper's highest grade. Forget lumpfish: The dye runs like mascara. The purist takes her caviar neat, spread on thin black bread or crackers. Drink as much chilled vodka or champagne as you like, because another magical property of caviar is acetylcholine, which *absorbs alcohol*. On New Year's or any old Eve, caviar elevates a plain dish into a dazzler. For brunch, pull out a box of frozen blini (buckwheat pancakes), nuke them, and let guests roll up their caviar with a dollop of crème fraîche or sour cream. A blow-em-away pasta course is fresh linguini tossed with olive oil, a smidge of pesto, and at the last minute—eggs, laid on gently. They break even easier than the chicken kind.

No silver spoons when dishing it out, or steel cutlery. It oxidizes the eggs and you taste the metal. Use mother of pearl and glass, even plastic. Caviar is also very perishable. Ideal storing temperature is 28 degrees (in the fridge in a plastic bag with ice). An unopened container should last a month. Once opened, no more than three days.

When shopping, be bold and ask for a taste. Up close, check to see that the eggs look pert—if they're smashed they were probably frozen or badly handled. Take a whiff. They should not smell fishy. Then crush them against the roof of your mouth to release the medley of flavors—briny, coppery, truffley. Look pensive, and try some more.

SPIRITS

The waitress is looking at you, kid. What's it gonna be? It's almost bedtime. You're stuffed to the gills, then you blurt out "gin and tonic," because you can't think of anything else. It's a free country, but that's a lame choice for an after-dinner drink. You know it, they know it, so why the heck did you just order one? Make a few spiritual journeys. When at a crossroads, go with the bottle less traveled.

Nooners

Pimms No. 1

British answer to a day spa is a few glasses of this herbal aromatherapy while watching the matches at Wimbledon. A "Pimm's cup," as it's called when served with cucumber and soda, is light on alcohol, which makes it a brilliant tipple for a long country afternoon, on the deck of a boat (the quinine helps you keep your sea legs), while playing croquet, or at any other fruity sporting event.

Campari

When mixed with soda this fizzy pink thirst quencher conjures the Riviera and is excellent on the bocce court. Recuperating from an Italian shoe-shopping spree and queasy from overspending? These bitters, a bark extract of the South American cinchona tree, will settle the stomach.

Pernod

A milder, gentler form of absinthe, the notorious liqueur that made Van Gogh chop off his ear and drove many great artistes to madness and early graves. The licorice-flavored pick-me-up was a favorite of American expats in Paris in the twenties. It goes with a splash of soda or rocks, especially when scribbling madly like Zelda Fitzgerald in a French café, or just feeling pretentious.

Bracers

Pear Williams

This colorless brandy distilled from the juice of fruits is a member of the eau de vie family. With the refined aroma of fruit blossoms, and fiery finish that will blowtorch the arteries after the Camembert, it makes a brisk nightcap. Also in the family is Williams's Swiss cousin Kirsch, a bit of cherry-flavored cheer to carry in your flask when chasing Hans down the slopes. Grappa is the Italian grandpapa made of grape skins and stems—and any other vineyard trash that wakes you from a manicotti stupor.

Sherry

For when Don Juan stops by for a nightcap and a late game of chess. Very Spanish (they make it) yet very English (they import it). The taste, like the hours the Spanish keep, is nutty. Good anytime, with a three o'clock snack, midnight dinner, or even later. It's oxidized wine, fortified with brandy, made in southern Spain, where they don't go in for the Harveys Bristol and other cream sherries—too frilly. Real bullfighters drink the drier kind, Manzanilla, Fino, Amontillado, Oloroso.

Port

Good and grapey, like Welch's for grown-ups, but keep that to yourself. The French (who drink it before dinner) and English (who drink it after) think it's classy. Produced in Portugal, it's like sherry, a wine exposed to oxygen and fortified with brandy during fermentation. Very alcoholic, best served in small, sweet doses.

Warning: This Passage May Stink.

Ilene: No one wanted to put cigars in this book except me. They said cigars are gross and ostentatious and smoked by jerks. But I am one of those jerks. And have been since I was a wee weed-hopper, secondhand-inhaling my dad's smoky treats as they commingled with his Christian Dior cologne. They're good comedy props, from Groucho to George Burns, who used his on stage instead of a watch. When it was burned halfway down, he knew it was time to get off. And they freshen up the air on the golf course or under the stars in front of a fire. That's where I smoke 'em.

The bigger and darker a cigar, the more potent. Judge the color by the outer leaf, or wrapper, which ranges from the light and mild "claro" to the blackest and meanest "oscuro." They're measured by length in inches; girth by ring size; and shape. Each shape has a different name: e.g., the Torpedo and the short, fat Robusto. On the other end of the spectrum is the long, thin, lady-size Panatela. The average-Joe, standby cigar is the Corona. If the wrapper is silky, veins delicate, and it's springy to the touch, the cigar was stored well, in a humidor at 70 degrees, or in Tupperware with a moist sponge in it (but not in a refrigerator, which dries them out).

Once you've selected one you like, "cap" the end with a guillotine. Too small a cut and the cigar will go out, too large a chop and one puff'll knock you out. To light, toast the end for a few seconds, like browning a marshmallow, then puff while rotating the cigar to light it evenly. Do not inhale, draw slowly. A cigar lasts between thirty to ninety minutes. You don't have to smoke the whole thing, but don't stab it out. It'll expire on its own. Then hang your clothes in a hefty bag with an open box of baking soda, so they don't keep smoking after you've quit.

Sometimes a drink-drink is just too much. But you want a little something anyway. Just a coffee. But while you're in there, jolt the joe with a splash of sambuca, Tia Maria, Fra Angelico. When sniffling, try a hot toddy: hot water, lemon, and honey, with a booster shot of whiskey. At the ski chalet, cocoa spruced up with a dash of Kahlúa. On second thought, make it Schnapps. Hans should be finishing his run soon.

DIAMONDS: YOU DO THE MATH

They're supposed to be your best friend, but how well do you really know them? Why wait 'til you get engaged? Break the ice early with a get-acquainted stud earring or a pendant necklace. Find a jeweler you can trust as much as your ace car mechanic. If the ice monkey's good, he'll tell you a diamond's like a painting and the setting is the frame. Don't blow your wad on the frame. He'll also tell you bigger is not necessarily better. Sure, they're sold by weight, measured in carats (5 carats equal one gram—big even for Liz Taylor), and expressed in decimals (1.25 cts, for instance, is quite a gem); but just because a Cadillac takes up more parking space, doesn't mean it looks better than a Maserati. What matters is that the style suits you and how much fire's under the hood. A loupe, which magnifies a diamond to ten times its actual size, will help determine the diamond's clarity, or how perfect it is. Don't get blinded by the specs. Flaws not visible to the human eye may affect a diamond's rareness but not necessarily its personality. You want to consider both when finding a pet rock to call your own. Take color, for example. The whiter or more colorless a diamond is, the rarer and more expensive. They're graded by letters, from D (least color) to Z (most yellow). But a diamond tinged with yellow can be more lively, especially in the right setting. The thing you can't screw around with is the cut. A diamond in the rough is not beautiful. It's up to the diamond cutter to cut and polish the stone to release its potential beauty. The proportions have to be right. Pick up a loupe, and check out a brilliant cut, or round, stone. Is the top (or crown) sloped, is the diameter (girdle) fatter on one side, does the bottom point (culet) look chipped? In fancy-shaped diamonds—pear, marquise, baguette, emerald, etc.—determining the quality of the cut is more subjective. Still, you can check to see if it's uniformly brilliant, or if there are dead spots (a darkened area across the center of the stone). Does it take your breath away? Does it make you start humming . . . "a kiss on the hand may be quite continental . . . But diamonds are a . . ."

FLOWERS

Cheaper than a cat, lower maintenance than plants. You might not have good art, or a view of any living thing, but flowers you can always afford. But since there's nothing more depressing than watching the pretty things die prematurely, keep them alive as long as you can with a few simple surgical maneuvers and conditioning products from your kitchen cabinet. Cutting flowers traumatizes them. You want to return them to their happier state. The more exposure to water the better. First, remove all the leaves and side shoots from the part of the stems that go underwater. This lets the flowers drink more and keeps the water clean. Recut the bottoms of most flowers on a slant (above the node), with the exception of tubular, strawlike stems like anemones, tulips, and daffodils; cut them straight across. After snipping, put the flowers in water immediately. Air clogs the pores, so to speak. Change water daily. To keep flowers looking bouncy and alive, they need as much trimming and conditioning as your hair. Before styling, try these overnight treatments.

Roses

Remove lower leaves and thorns. Immersing them in a small amount of boiling water forces buds open and preserves the blooms. Then put in lukewarm water up to first thorns or leaves (for one gallon of water, two tablespoons salt or a pouch of florists' Chrysal powder). Dip the ends of the stems in some melted sealing wax and they'll stay sassy even out of the water for hours.

Tulips

Place in a small amount of warm water with one half teaspoon sugar to one quart water. To keep from bending, roll in wet newspaper, then submerge in cold water up to the head.

Iris and daisies

Treat with three drops of peppermint oil in a quart of water.

Lilacs

Scrape bark off bottom of the branch, smash the end with a hammer, fray, and soak in cold water with Chrysal powder.

Lilies

One half cup vinegar per gallon of water.

Mmmmmm, Looks Good Enough to Eat

Fried zucchini blossoms

This Italian summer treat is hard to come by because the bright orange flowers that look like baby tiger lilies are so fragile. If you ever see them at a green-market, buy as many as they'll sell. If you spot some growing beside the squash plants in a garden patch, slam on the brakes, steal as many as you can carry. Once home, shake them free of bugs, stuff a bit of mozzarella or anchovy in the center; mix flour and milk so that it forms a thin batter, dip the stuffed flower in the batter, and sauté in hot oil. Worth the risk of prison.

Vodka still-life

Gertrude Stein's fun-loving companion, Alice B. Toklas, liked to experiment not only with magic herbs but with flowers. Place a half pound of petals of carnations, violets, and orange blossoms, along with a clove, a stick of cinnamon, and a quart of vodka in a jar. Let infuse for a month. Then strain through coffee filters. Add sugar to taste.

OYSTERS

Slurping oysters from the shell is the closest thing you can have to sex in a public restaurant. If you're gonna do it, ignore your inhibitions and get down and dirty. But be safe! A little knowledge will help minimize the health risks and enhance your pleasure. Take a pamphlet from Planned Oysterhood. A few myths, and facts, every crustaceously active girl should know:

They're bad for you

A bad one will make you sicker than a landlubber in a winter squall. Healthy

oysters should be plump and flesh-colored (not look like a flat tire), with a briny water, called "liquor," and smell sweet. They're the richest animal source of vitamins and minerals, high in phosphorous, iron, copper, and iodine, and vitamin D—alleged to increase sexual desire.

They're an aphrodisiac

No one's proved it, but Casanova ate fifty a day. He must have known something.

They can only be eaten during months with the letter *R*.

This warning not to eat oysters in summer started with conservationists in the twenties. They didn't want people farming oysters from May to September when they reproduce. During these months, when they're laying eggs, isn't the ideal time to eat them anyway, because their meat can be more gooey, lean, and watery. But order them any time you want, except if you think they might have been left out for hours in a sweltering kitchen or hot summer sun. In Parisian brasseries, they leave the muscle uncut, so a fresh squeeze of lemon or turn of pepper still makes them flinch. Sadly, the freshness test won't work at many American eateries, where they cut the muscle and flip the oyster in its shell to make it look pretty.

All oysters are created equal

The waiter rattles off the list—Blue Points, Chesapeakes, Malpeques—and you think, *How different can they be?* As different as the seas that spawn them: the Mediterranean and the Atlantic, Chesapeake Bay and the Gulf of Mexico.

Here's an assorted platter:

- Malpeques: Small and easy to stomach for the novice, from Prince Edward Island, nicely bitter, like lettuce, pointed oblong shell.

- Belons: The president of oysters, traditionally European is now found around the world, known for being sweet and salty and very intense, round flat shell.

- Wellfleet: From Wellfleet, Cape Cod, with a pleasantly salty and beachy clean flavor, oval shell.

- Kumamoto: Don't be scared of the green tint, these itty-bitty oysters, indigenous to Japan now farmed in California, taste fruity and are smooth as butta.

- Portuguese oysters: The variety Hemingway loved to eat in Paris cafés in the twenties, can now be found in Vancouver and the Pacific Northwest. They're big and nutty, good for cooking, and a macho choice when ordered raw, green ruffled shell.

- Blue Points: Once the ultimate New York oyster, today they're no longer produced and the term refers to the average mild Atlantic oyster.

You look stupid eating them

Not if you've got the technique down. Dip your fish fork in the cocktail sauce and dab the oyster. At a fancy place, you might want to raise the shell with one hand and fork the meat with your other. Otherwise, just lift the broad end of the shell to your lips and slide the sucker down whole, the "liquor," too. Oyster shooters, "drinking" them out of shot glasses, is the equivalent of doing it on the kitchen floor. To wash them down, you don't necessarily need the greatest white wine if the oysters are good: It'll steal the show (something between muscadet and muscatel). The English swallow them with a mixture of champagne and stout. But never mix with whiskey, brandy, or any other strong spirits: They react in the stomach in strange and unpleasant ways that, without going into gory details, let's just say are something of an antiaphrodisiac.

SINGLE MALT SCOTCH

"Strong, salty, peaty, woody, quite layered, with a high-toned nose, oaky notes, and a rich finish." People now natter on about scotch with the fruity verbosity of wine aficionados and pay as much for a glass as for a whole bottle of vino. We're not talking about the kind you see ordered with soda and a twist. That's blended scotch. Single malts are a whole other world.

In Scotland, there are as many distilleries as vineyards in Bordeaux, and what they don't slough off to blend manufacturers, they keep to make the really good stuff—in small quantities. For it to be single malt it must be made from one hundred percent malted barley (with no grain whiskey mixed in) from a single distillery and then aged anywhere from three to twenty-five years in oak casks tended to by little old Scottish men in wool hats who disagree violently and proudly about the correct methodology.

All kinds of things affect flavor, from the spring water used to soak the barley to the still's size, shape, and condition as well as the fairies and monsters in their lochs.

To order scotch from a menu means overcoming the crazy pronunciations. The name of the scotch includes the region, which tells you a lot about how it'll taste. Follow the River Spey, which runs through the Highlands, where the soil is rich and the scotch probably too peaty for your blood:

- Speyside: A valley chockablock with distilleries that make sweet and light-bodied malts.
- Livet: A tributary of Spey, home of Glenlivet, the first whiskey, and all the "Glen" whiskeys that followed (deep mellowness and delicate aroma, not too peaty).
- Islay (eye-lah): An island off the western coast notorious for the most heavily peated, pungent, and weightiest of scotch.

All of it is at least 40 percent alcohol, so sip slowly. And don't swirl.

TRUFFLES: NOT THE CHOCOLATES

In Italy and France—motherlands of the white and black truffle, respectively—you'd think the stubby underground mushrooms were illegal, the way people behave during their all-too-short season. They sell them from the backs of cars. The famous truffle market in Alba is like a drug bazaar, with dealers measuring out their merch on gram scales and keeping the best stuff in their pockets for the hungriest and highest-paying addicts. Adding to their contraband allure, truffles are still dug up under cover of night, when their odor is strongest and to shake spies. Armed with a flashlight and a pickax called a *zappeta*, the truffle hunter seeks out the young oaks under which truffles grow and roots them out with dogs or pigs who can sniff out a twelve-inch-deep truffle from twenty feet away.

Always associated with decadence and excess, truffles were prohibited in Roman times, but ancient swells secretly consumed them in speakeasies. Now that they're legal, take advantage of these rare, narcotically delicious delicacies, whose musky scent has been compared to garlic, cheese, and an unmade bed. (Testosterase, a substance akin to the male sex hormone, gives truffles their sexy smell.) This triple-X experience hardly seems appropriate for a restaurant, where you pay a month's rent for truffle risotto. They barely wave the thing over your plate and all you can think is, *Gimme more!* The only way to be truly satisfied is to indulge at home, where you can get more bang for your buck.

Buy the black ones in fall, the wetter the season the better. The best of them are Perigord, named after their region in southwest France, where they call them Black Diamonds. Used for cooking, they come packed in rice. Shards of the shrooms can stuff a chicken or electrify mashed potatoes. Italian white truffles

Licking the Label

A label is a vintner's place to boast (a résumé). The more he's got to brag about, the more information on the bottle. If it just says "Càbernet Sauvignon" it's generic. But if it says "Château Saint Papillon/Premier cru, mise en bouteille au château/Bordeaux," they're telling you this is not just any bottle, it's from the famous Bordeaux-making town of Saint Papillon, and, even better, it's bottled at the vineyard's own château. The more information, the closer you're getting to the vintner's private stash. Code words that you're getting close: "Premier Cru" (first growth), therefore they're older grapes, a good thing. "Grand Cru" is as good as it gets; "Château" or "Reserve" usually indicates a cut above the rest of the wine the vineyard produces. "Les" or "Clos" something are also words to look out for. And if Baron de Rothschild's name appears anywhere, buy it, no matter how much it costs.

- Glasses: Clear glass lets you see the color of the wine. That's helpful since a way to tell if red wine is ready is to hold it against the menu. Red wines get lighter in color as they age, so if you can see the letters on the menu through the vino, it's good to go. Glasses should curve in at the rim to contain the aroma. But a juice glass works too, especially if it's a table wine, because then it's like you're in a trattoria in Italy.
- Chilling: Like with champagne, the most efficient way of chilling wine is in icy water. (An eight-minute dunk will bring temp down from 65 to 55.) To speed-chill while traveling, wrap bottle in a wet newspaper or cloth and hold it by the open car window.

If you make a good choice, ask them to give you the label.

are only available until November and are eaten raw. Shave off paper-thin pieces with a mandolin into anything from a salad to a bowl of pasta with butter. Any way you slice 'em turns a normal dish into a meal that makes you moan. Beware, they are said to provoke wild dreams—*or were they dreams?*

WINE

The best response to a snooty sommelier is to sample a bottle of wine like a pro. After he's presented you with the label and poured you a taste, raise the glass by the stem, swirl (to release the bouquet), take a long inhale, nod approval to the waiter, and say "*Magnifique!*" The professional wine tasters of the world couldn't possibly taste every wine, so they do the sniff test. If it smells like sulfur, mold, or something you'd toss salad with, it may have turned. That's the only really justifiable reason to send it back. If you gamble on a Canadian rosé, and it smells like a lumberjack's cologne—that's your problem. Chalk it up to a learning experience. As an oenophile you are a student of your own taste. A good wine is simply a matter of what you like and what you don't. Learn your palate. Hold a taste on your tongue for a minute: A tingle on the sides is acid, sweetness is on the tip, and tannin makes the top dry out. It takes about forty-five seconds before swallowing to get a sense of how all those components affect the general fruitiness of the wine. You can apply this taste test every time. Soon you'll understand that if you're the only person you know who hates California chardonnay, it's probably from the tannin in the oaky barrels (or that's added artificially to make the wine taste aged). And if you like pinot noir even more than more expensive merlots, it's because you prefer the taste of acid and fruit to tannin.

BONBON VOYAGE

Friends, do you recognize this image? A forlorn young woman in her prime sitting alone in the dark, drowning her despond in a tub of Double-Chocolate Dee-lite, a tray of brownies on one side, an open can of frosting on the other. When did guilt, post-dump depression, or general malaise become chocolate's dark companions? Let's reassess our relationship with nature's answer to Prozac.

Chocolate contains phenylethylamine, an endorphin-activating chemical the brain releases when we fall in love—or do a spinning class. Eat twenty-five pounds or more and it'll have the same effects as marijuana. But that doesn't mean only use it when your mood is blacker than bittersweet Toblerone. Can't we get back to the glorious gluttony of youth? Reconnect with the days when a chocolate bar from the corner store seemed to promise an afternoon of delight and endless possibilities?

Imagine you won the "golden ticket" and act out those latent Willy Wonka fantasies. Make up an excuse occasion—A Friend Just Got a New Dog Day, or Boyfriend's Too Skinny Week—to do something sweet. This requires overcoming any fear of wax paper, parchment, and double boilers. Concoct your own Whitman sampler, with strange, tasty confections made from whatever you want, no maple creams or any of those gross flavors you bite and throw back into the box. Feel Candyman Sammy Davis Jr. beaming on you from that big Candyland in the sky: "Talk about your childhood wishes. You could even eat the dishes. . . ."

Treat chocolate like gold. Melt it down and make it into something new. Melt pieces of Lindt, Hershey, Frango mints, last year's Easter bunny in a double boiler, or metal bowl over boiling water, over low heat. No direct flame or it'll burn. Thin it out with Crisco if it's too goopey, but not butter or margarine and definitely NOT water. Water is kryptonite to chocolate. Even a few drops will make it "seize," or coagulate. If that happens, nothing can bring back its velvety texture. Toss it and start over! Add one tablespoon of shortening per four ounces chocolate. Now dip. Cherries, pretzel nuggets, jelly bean clusters, Chuckle Rings, caramels, Swedish fish, a dried apricot, the head of a tiny spoon to stir your coffee, Rice Krispies, a pacifier, popcorn, dirty fortune cookies. Because as Willy said to Charlie, "You know what happened to the boy who suddenly got everything he wanted." She lived happily ever after.

PHOTO BY KEN SCHLASS

134

Conclusion
That's not all, folks...

All right, we've given you everything we got, all the stuff we know and a lot we had to look up. There are probably a zillion things we'll wake up tomorrow and slap our foreheads for forgetting. But, as you know by now, a swell isn't perfect. You probably have a few thoughts on this subject, too, which is good, because by now you oughtta be imagining your own swell world. After all, that's the point. This book is not a paint-by-numbers kit. Hopefully, there are a couple of ideas in here worth lifting and a bit of useful info. But it's all designed to help give you the guts to try some things you might not have before—to do things your own way. What's swell or isn't is up to you. Just because we wrote a book and shared some personal history doesn't mean we have all the answers. Our liptotes aren't always in order. Swellness is as much our fantasy as reality: a fun idea of cruising through life in the fast lane, thinking big thoughts, taking time for small acts of duking. But now you're behind the wheel, so step on the gas! And don't worry if you blow a tire—you know how to change it. Have a swell trip!

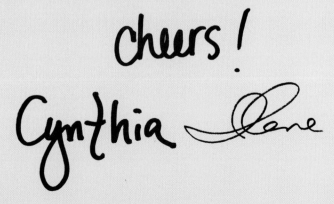

cheers!

Cynthia Rowe

Sources

The following books were helpful in our quest to provide useful information for the education of a Swell.

- *A Woman's Guide to Cigar Smoking*, Rhona Kaspar, St. Martin's Press, April 1998
- *All About Chocolate*, Carole Bloom, Macmillan, 1998
- *The American Girl's Handy Book*, Lena Beard and Adelia Beard, Nonpareil Book, 1987
- *Caruso and the Art of Singing*, Salvatore Fucito and Barnet J. Beyer, Dover Publications, 1995
- *Cary Grant: A Class Apart*, Graham McCann, Columbia University Press, 1996
- *Cocktail: The Drinks Bible for the 21st Century*, Paul Harrington and Laura Moorehead, Viking, 1998
- *Consider the Oyster*, M. F. K. Fisher, North Point Press, 1988 (third printing, 1996)
- *Crowning Glory: Reflections of Hollywood's Favorite Confidante*, Sydney Guilaroff, General Publishing Group, 1996
- *Edible Flowers*, Claire Clifton, McGraw Hill Books, 1983
- *Esquire's Handbook for Hosts*, Grosset and Dunlap, 1949
- *Fabulous Fragrances*, Jan Moran, Crescent House Publishing, 1994
- *The Flowers of La Grenouille*, Charles Masson, Clarkson Potter Publishers, 1994
- *Food*, Waverly Root, Smithmark Publishers, 1996
- *The Food Lover's Tiptionary*, Sharon Tyler Herbst, Hearst Books, 1994
- *Frank Sinatra*, John Howlett, Plexus Publishing, 1980
- *High Spirits: A Celebration of Scotch, Bourbon, Cognac, and More*, H. Paul Jeffers, Lyons and Buford, 1997
- *How to Buy Jewelry Wholesale*, Frank J. Adler, House of Collectibles/The Ballantine Publishing Group, 1998
- *How to Enjoy Wine*, Hugh Johnson, Fireside, 1985
- *How to Talk Golf*, Dawson Taylor, Dembner Books, 1985
- *How to Win at Casino Games*, Belinda Levez, Teach Yourself Books, 1997
- *Lots of Luck*, Emily Gwathmey, Angel City Press, 1994
- *Lucille's Car Care*, Lucille Teganowan, Hyperion, 1996
- *The New Magician's Manual*, Walter B. Gibson, Dover Publications, 1975
- *The New Games Treasury*, Merilyn Simonds Mohr, Houghton Mifflin Company, 1997
- *Oysters: A Connoisseur's Guide and Cookbook*, Lonnie Williams and Karen Warner, Ten Speed Press, 1990
- *Oysters: A True Delicacy*, Shirley Line, MacMillan, 1995
- *Single Malt Scotch and Whiskey*, Daniel Lerner, Black Dog and Leventhal Publishers, 1997
- *Vocal Wisdom: Maxims of Giovanni Battista Lamperti*, Taplinger Publishing Company, 1931
- *The Way You Wear Your Hat: Frank Sinatra and the Lost Art of Living*, Bill Zehme, HarperCollins, 1997
- *Winning Pool Tips*, Steve Mizerak, VGM Career Horizons, 1995
- *Windows on the World Complete Wine Course*, Kevin Zraly, Sterling Publishing, 1998